Ideals presents

The Active Woman's Cookbook

Great tasting, time saving, money saving recipes!

Introduction

Saving time and money are the most important concerns for the active woman today.

Years ago, a woman might have spent all day in the kitchen. Today she directs her valuable resources and energies into multiple roles and expresses her talents as a career woman, sportswoman, and volunteer in the community, as well as a mother and wife.

Now, more than ever before, the active woman needs a helping hand around the home . . . especially in the kitchen. She is more aware of her family's nutritional needs, yet she has less time for shopping and meal preparation, and rising costs may leave less money in her budget to provide her family with the best food.

The Active Woman's Cookbook is the best "helping hand" you've ever had in your kitchen. We'll show you how to use seasonal "best buys" to your advantage, how to prepare a week of nutritious, delicious family meals on a low budget, how to grow herbs and use them in economical and creative dishes, and how to prepare a gourmet company meal in less than 60 minutes.

You've never had so much valuable information in one book before!

And, it is more than "just a cookbook"! The Active Woman's Cookbook includes information especially for you as a woman. Our "looking good" section gives important beauty, nutritional and diet information, and low-calorie recipes to keep you looking and feeling your best.

What are the results of using all this time and money-saving information and enjoying our delicious meals? You'll find that you have more time to spend doing the things *you* enjoy.

Contents

IDEALS PUBLISHING CORP. • Milwaukee, WI
Copyright © 1980 by Ideals Publishing Corp.
All rights reserved. Printed in the U.S.A.

The Key is Organization

Planning Your Pantry

Organization . . . the essential key to successfully coping with today's active lifestyle. Here are basic guidelines for planning and stocking your pantry, efficiently organizing your kitchen and planning your own time while incorporating meal preparation into your schedule. Once this is accomplished, you hold the essential key for saving both money and time in your active lifestyle.

A pantry . . . a storehouse of confidence at your fingertips. A basic stock can be your best friend in terms of last minute company, a weather emergency or the salad that doesn't look just right.

We've suggested a sample pantry of staple foods for you that include starches, sweets, condiments, canned or bottled items, and perishable goods, all pictured at the right. Most of the dry items, such as the pasta, beans, and rice are available in bulk quantities and have a long shelf life. Once purchased, they will last for six months or more. Other items, such as the perishable foods, may have to be replenished on your weekly shopping trip.

Basic starches we suggest having on hand, in addition to the usual flour and cornmeal, are several types of pasta, white and brown rice, various types of potatoes (red potatoes are especially versatile, as they can be boiled, roasted in their skins, or incorporated into potato salad in a minimum amount of cooking time) and dried beans. All of the above can be used as the basis for any entrée (Speedy Spinach Lasagne), as a side dish for a main course (Wild Rice) or as a hearty addition to soups and stews (Spiced Kettle of Beef and Vegetables).

Sweet-based staple items we've included are honey, maple syrup, brown and white sugars (for glazes on meats, vegetables and desserts), and jams and jellies, which can turn omelets or pancakes into an extra special dish anytime.

Favorite condiments (you may be more elaborate if you choose) begin with ketchup, yellow and brown mustard, olives, pickles and capers. In addition to topping the usual hamburger, try incorporating pickles into tuna fish salad for added crunch!

Other necessary shelf items are vegetable and olive oil, vinegar, Tabasco sauce and Worcestershire sauce. These items can be used in marinades, dressings, soups and stews, giving a particular dish added flavor and your own special touch. We've also included a can of tuna fish in this category as a representative of the tinned fish and meat items that may be stocked for easy sandwiches, salads, dips, casseroles and omelets.

Certain perishable foods can be considered staple items as they may be used in many dishes for almost any meal. Among these are garlic, green, yellow and white onions, green peppers, tomatoes, celery, lemons, eggs, cheese and nuts. From breakfast to dessert, you will find these items welcome helpers in meal preparation.

Planning Your Kitchen

A well-planned kitchen is the envy of all those whose kitchens are an obstacle course to efficient cooking. However, no matter how large or small, any kitchen can be tailored to suit your lifestyle if thought is given to your cooking habits and needs.

1. Invest in a good selection of pans and utensils to accomplish your culinary pursuits. A set of pans should include a 10-inch skillet with lid, an 8- to 10-inch omelet pan, a set of covered casseroles (freezer-to-oven ware is good), a roasting pan with rack, bread pans, two cookie sheets, a stockpot, a double-boiler, a teakettle, and a coffee maker.

2. Basic utensils begin with a set of good knives. Be sure to include a steel (sharpener) for proper maintenance of your investment. Other necessary items are: a set of measuring cups and spoons, a mallet for

tenderizing less expensive cuts of meat, a set of wooden spoons, spatula, shears, rolling pin, pastry blender and board, vegetable peeler, sieve, chop block, can opener, mortar and pestle for grinding herbs and spices, cleaver, cheese slicer, and tongs.

3. Gadgets include some of the larger items necessary to the cook's survival. Among these useful tools are a grater, sifter, colander, lettuce dryer, vegetable steamer, food grinder, a set of molds, egg beater, and whisk.

4. Other mainstays for an efficient kitchen are a mixer, blender, toaster, and a set of stainless steel or porcelain mixing bowls. A food processor, microwave oven and freezer are money- and time-saving investments.

5. Plan a logical workspace for yourself and be sure that all utensils have a definite place. For example, if you bake a lot, it is a good idea to set aside counterspace or a mobile kitchen worktable as a baking center. Your mixer, baking pans, utensils, and cannisters should be readily accessible to that area. A lettuce dryer should be kept adjacent to the sink so it isn't necessary to carry wet greens across the room. Think through your daily work pattern and plan your space accordingly.

Planning Your Time

You are perhaps the most important factor in saving money and time in your particular lifestyle. A basic pantry and an organized kitchen are invaluable tools to an active cook, but you can make the most of your resources by following these suggestions:

1. Plan a weekly menu and then make your shopping list according to the menu. Add those staples which you have run low on. Completely filling your list every week will not only save time, but will also save gas.

2. Avoid trips to the store for a single item.

3. *Never* go to the store hungry . . . you may be tempted to deviate from your list.

4. Plan a timetable for meal preparation so the green beans are not done ten minutes before the chicken and lose color, texture, flavor, and nutritive value.

5. If you have conveniences such as a microwave oven or food processor, take advantage of them and incorporate them into planning your time schedule and menu for the week.

Weights and Measures

1 tbsp	3 tsp	15mL
1 fl oz	2 tbsp	30mL
¼ cup	4 tbsp	50mL
⅓ cup	5⅓ cup	75mL
½ cup	8 tbsp	125mL
⅔ cup	10⅔ tbsp	150-175mL
¾ cup	12 tbsp	175-200mL
1 cup	16 tbsp or 8 fl oz	250mL
1 pt	2½ cups	625mL
1 qt	2½ pts or 5 cups	1.25L
1 lb	16 ozs	500g
¾ lb	12 ozs	350g
½ lb	8 ozs	250g
¼ lb	4 ozs	125g

Equivalent Amounts

Apples, 3 med	1 lb	500g
Baking Chocolate, 1 sq grated	1 oz or 5 tbsp	3g or 75mL
Bread	1 lb loaf	500g loaf
Butter or Margarine, 1 stick	1 lb = 2 cups ¼ lb = ½ cup	500g = 500mL 125g = 125mL
Cheese, grated	1 lb = 4 cups	500g = 1L
Cottage Cheese	1 lb = 2 cups	500g = 500mL
Eggs, 5 whole 8 whites 16 yolks	1 cup about 1 cup about 1 cup	250mL about 250mL about 250mL
Flour, all-purpose	1 lb = 4 cups	500g = 1L
Flour, cake	1 lb = 4¾ cups	500g = 1.2L
Lemon juice, 1 med lemon	3 tbsp juice	45mL juice
Lemon rind, 1 med lemon	1 tbsp	15mL
Noodles	1 cup raw = 1¼ cups cooked	250mL raw = 300mL cooked
Macaroni	1 lb = 3 cups uncooked 1 cup = 2 cups cooked	500g = 750mL uncooked 250 mL = 500 mL cooked
Meat, diced	2 cups = 1 lb	500mL = 500g
Milk, evaporated, canned	one 6 oz = ⅔ cup one 14 oz. = 1⅔ cups	one 160 mL one 385mL
Potatoes, 3 med	1 lb	500g
Rice	1 lb = 2⅓ cups uncooked 1 cup raw = 3 cups cooked	500g = 575mL uncooked 250mL raw = 725mL cooked
Sugar, Brown, firmly packed Confectioners' Granulated	1 lb = 2¼ cups 1 lb = 3½ cups 1 lb = 2 cups	500g = 550mL 500g = 875 mL 500g = 500mL
Tomatoes, 3 med	1 lb	500g
Shortening	1 lb = 2 cups	500g = 500mL

Saving Money

- Best Buys of the Season
- A Week of Budget Dinners
- Hearty Meals in a Dish
- Add Flavor and Lower Cost with Herbs
- Winning Ways with Meat
- Variations on a Theme

Every consumer today needs to be concerned with getting the most out of her food dollar. The following chapters were designed with that fact in mind to offer you delicious recipes with which to stretch your budget.

In addition to our recipes, here are some tips to keep in mind when planning the weekly menu and selecting items on your list:

1. Seasonal produce is your best buy. Green beans in season cost less per serving than do canned. Also, fresh produce has better flavor, fewer additives and greater nutritional value than processed food.

2. High ticket items are placed at eye level. Check the top and bottom shelves for similar items with lower price tags.

3. A word to the butcher now and then may give you advance notice of sales to help you plan the weekly budget accordingly.

4. Avoid impulse buying. If it is not on your list, don't buy it!

5. Stay within your budget; a small notepad or pocket calculator can help.

6. Take advantage of coupons, but be wise! Only buy the product if it is already on your shopping list.

7. Check local newspapers for weekly sales. A dozen cans of tuna fish at a great sale price mean big savings and can be stored indefinitely. Eggs, stored in their cartons will last four to five weeks (Figure this savings into your long-term budget; pay now and save for weeks to come.).

8. Buy cheese such as Swiss and Cheddar in bricks. Slice at home and save the cost of handling and packaging.

9. Compare! Notice the difference in the price per pound of boneless chicken breasts and whole breasts with ribs; fillets peel right off the bone after par-boiling for 10 to 12 minutes and are only about one-half the price of boned chicken breasts.

10. Vegetable trimmings make flavorful additions to soups and stews. Stretch the recipes and liven the flavor by adding a little water and a few bouillon cubes.

11. Turn not-quite-fresh bread and crackers into crumbs for use in stuffing, casseroles and meatloaf. Just put them in the blender.

12. Save the oil from deep-frying. Strain through cheesecloth and keep refrigerated.

13. Citrus fruit yields more juice at room temperature.

Spring

Fruits and Vegetables March-May

Inexpensive		**Affordable**
Artichokes	Rhubarb	Apples
Asparagus	Spinach	Avocados
Bananas	Squash	Beans
Broccoli	Tomatoes	Beets
Cabbage		Brussels Sprouts
Carrots		Cauliflower
Celery		Corn
Cucumbers		Eggplant
Grapefruit		Limes
Lemons		Mushrooms
Lettuce		Peaches
Onions		Pears
Oranges		Strawberries
Peppers		
Pineapples		
Potatoes		
Radishes		

Salads

Chef's Super Salad with Garlic Dressing

    1 head lettuce, shredded
    2 cups spinach, torn into bite-sized pieces
    1 cup cooked ham, slivered
    1 cup cooked turkey, slivered
    ¼ pound pepperoni, thinly sliced
    ¼ pound sharp Cheddar cheese, slivered
    ¼ pound Danish havarti with caraway, slivered
    1 small green pepper, diced
    1 medium cucumber, thinly sliced
    2 hard-cooked eggs, quartered
    8 cherry tomatoes, sliced
    ½ cup croutons

Chill greens until ready to serve. Just before serving, arrange greens on platter. Place the remaining ingredients upon the greens in an attractive pattern. Serves 4 as a main dish.

Garlic Dressing

    ¾ cup olive or vegetable oil
    ¼ cup wine vinegar
    ½ teaspoon salt
       Freshly ground black pepper to taste
    1 clove garlic, minced (optional)

Mix all ingredients together thoroughly. Taste and correct seasoning. 1 cup.

Salade Nicoise with Vinaigrette Dressing

    4 potatoes, cooked, peeled, and sliced
       Mayonnaise
    3 to 4 ripe tomatoes, quartered
    3 cups lightly steamed green beans
    1 7-ounce can white tuna, drained and flaked
    ½ cup olives
    1 medium red onion, thinly sliced
    1 green pepper, deseeded and sliced into rounds
    3 stalks celery, sliced
    3 hard-boiled eggs, quartered
    1 head Boston lettuce leaves
       Vinaigrette Dressing
    ½ cup minced parsley
    1 tablespoon fresh chopped basil
    ½ teaspoon chopped chives
       Anchovies

Mix enough mayonnaise with potatoes to coat thoroughly. Toss tomatoes lightly in a small amount of Vinaigrette Dressing. In a separate bowl, toss green beans in a small amount of Vinaigrette Dressing. Let marinate while preparing the rest of the salad; drain before adding to salad. When ready to serve, toss lettuce lightly in a small amount of Vinaigrette Dressing until leaves are barely coated. Place around the edge and bottom of the bowl, using all the leaves. Place tuna in the center of the bowl; arrange tomatoes, green beans, and potatoes around the outside in an interesting pattern. Decorate with olives, onion slices, green pepper rounds, celery, and eggs. Garnish with herbs and anchovies. Serve immediately with additional Vinaigrette Dressing. 8 servings.

Vinaigrette Dressing

    ¼ cup wine vinegar (or part lemon juice)
    ¾ cup olive or vegetable oil
    ¼ teaspoon salt
    ½ teaspoon dry mustard
       Freshly ground black pepper
    1 teaspoon minced parsley
    1 teaspoon minced sweet basil
    1 large clove garlic, minced (optional)

Place all ingredients in a jar; cover tightly and shake thoroughly. Shake again just before using. 1 cup.

Chef's Salad with Garlic Dressing
Broccoli Casserole p. 8
Tangy Fruitcake p. 9

Fresh Mushroom Salad

3 tablespoons fresh lemon juice
⅔ cup olive oil
3 tablespoons wine vinegar
1½ teaspoons salt
¾ teaspoon pepper
3 cloves garlic, minced
10 to 12 cups mixed greens
1 pound mushrooms, thinly sliced
1 cup croutons

Place lemon juice, oil, vinegar, salt, pepper, and garlic in a jar; shake well and refrigerate. Prepare greens and mushrooms in salad bowl. Bring dressing to room temperature and shake well before pouring over greens and mushrooms. Sprinkle with croutons. Makes 6 to 8 servings.

Vegetables

Glazed Carrots

1 pound carrots, scrubbed, peeled, cut in strips or slices
Salt and pepper
½ cup orange marmalade
¼ cup butter
1 tablespoon mint jelly (optional)

In a saucepan, cover carrots with water; add salt and pepper to taste. Cook until barely tender; drain. Melt butter with marmalade and jelly, stirring until all are blended. Add carrots and cook together for a few minutes. Serves 4 to 6.

Hollandaise Sauce for Vegetables

½ cup margarine or butter
3 egg yolks at room temperature
1½ tablespoons lemon juice
¼ teaspoon dry mustard
¼ teaspoon salt
Freshly ground black pepper

In a small saucepan, melt butter until bubbly. Place egg yolks, lemon juice, mustard, and seasonings into blender container; cover and blend on low until yolks are frothy. Pour in half the butter in a very slow, steady stream until creamy. Then turn blender to high and add remaining butter slowly. Taste and correct seasonings. Serve immediately on steamed vegetables such as Brussels sprouts, broccoli, zucchini. If reheated, warm the sauce gently over hot water, stirring carefully. 1 cup.

Broccoli Casserole

3 to 4 cups chopped broccoli
⅓ cup finely chopped onion
4 tablespoons margarine
3 tablespoons whole wheat pastry flour
½ cup vegetable cooking water or broth
¾ cup grated Cheddar cheese
3 eggs, well-beaten
½ cup whole wheat bread crumbs
1 tablespoon butter or margarine

Preheat oven to 325°. Melt 4 tablespoons margarine in a large skillet over medium heat; stir in onion and broccoli; sauté covered, until broccoli is barely tender. (If using frozen broccoli, drop about 20 ounces into a small amount of boiling water, cover, and cook quickly. Add to skillet and use the cooking water later in the recipe.) Stir flour into the onion-broccoli mixture and let cook a minute or so. Add cooking water or broth; stir until thickened. Lower heat and quickly stir in cheese until well blended. Remove from heat and gradually stir in eggs. Pour into a well greased 1½ to 2-quart casserole. Pour crumbs over and dot with butter. Bake for 30 minutes or until done. 8 servings.

Asparagus Oriental

1 tablespoon vegetable oil
2 thin slices fresh gingerroot
3 cups fresh asparagus
½ teaspoon salt
Pepper to taste
¼ cup toasted almonds (optional)

Heat skillet or wok; add oil and gingerroot. When ginger is hot, remove. Slice asparagus, on a slant, in 1½-inch slices; add to oil. Sprinkle with salt and pepper and cover. Lift skillet slightly above heat and shake constantly while cooking. Cook 4 to 5 minutes until crisp tender. Add toasted almonds if desired. Serves 2 to 4.

Cauliflower Moiré

1 head cauliflower
½ cup sour cream
1 tablespoon prepared mustard
¼ teaspoon salt
¼ teaspoon pepper
2 to 3 green onions, snipped

Steam or cook cauliflower for about 20 minutes until just tender. Combine remaining ingredients. Heat but do not boil. Pour over hot cauliflower and sprinkle with paprika. Serves 6 to 8.

Desserts

Lemon Fromage

    3 eggs
    2 egg yolks
    ½ cup sugar
       Grated rind of 1 lemon
       Juice of 2 lemons
    1 tablespoon gelatin
    ½ pint heavy cream, whipped stiff
       Strawberries (optional garnish)

Beat whole eggs and yolks until light and frothy. Gradually add sugar and beat until thick. Add rind. Soften gelatin in lemon juice and dissolve over hot water. When cool, add to egg mixture, beating well. Fold in whipped cream and pour into a 1-quart melon mold or bowl. Chill about 4 hours or until firm. Unmold and serve with garnish of berries and whipped cream if desired.

Orange Rind Cake

    1   cup raisins
    ½   cup nuts
        Rind of 2 oranges
    1   cup sugar
    ½   cup butter
    2   eggs
    1   cup buttermilk
    1   teaspoon baking soda
    2½ cups flour
        Confectioners' sugar

Put raisins, nuts and rind through a grinder. Set aside. Cream butter with sugar; stir in eggs and buttermilk, mixing well. Add soda, flour and ground mixture. Pour batter into a greased and floured bundt pan. Bake in a 350° oven 45 to 60 minutes. Serves 10 to 12. Dust with confectioners' sugar.

Rhubarb Cream Pie

    1½ cups sugar
    3   tablespoons flour
    1   teaspoon nutmeg
    1½ tablespoons butter
    2   eggs, well-beaten
    3   cups cut rhubarb
        Pastry for double-crust pie (page 17)

Blend sugar, flour, nutmeg and butter. Add eggs; beat until smooth; pour over rhubarb in 9-inch pastry-lined pie pan. Top with pastry. Bake at 450° for 10 minutes, then at 350° about 30 minutes. Serve warm or cooled.

Quick Pineapple Coffee Cake

    1½ cups sifted all-purpose flour
    2   teaspoons baking powder
    ¼   teaspoon salt
    2   tablespoons sugar
    1   egg
    ½   cup milk
    ⅓   cup shortening, melted
    ⅓   cup fresh pineapple,
        diced and well drained
    2   tablespoons honey
    1   tablespoon butter, melted
    3   tablespoons chopped pecans

Sift together flour, baking powder, salt and sugar. Beat egg; add milk and cooled shortening. Pour into flour mixture; stir only until dry ingredients are moistened. Turn into greased and floured 8-inch round layer cake pan. Mix pineapple, honey and butter together. Spoon pineapple topping over batter. Sprinkle nuts on top. Bake in preheated 400° oven 30 minutes. Serve warm. Serves 8.

Tangy Fruitcake

    ½   cup butter
    ¾   cup sugar
    2   eggs
    1   tablespoon lemon rind
    1   teaspoon lemon extract
    1⅔ cups sifted cake flour
    1½ teaspoons baking powder
    ¼   teaspoon salt
    ⅔   cup milk
        Confectioners' sugar
        Sliced and sweetened strawberries
        Heavy cream, whipped

Cream butter and sugar until light and fluffy. Beat in eggs, one at a time, beating well after each addition. Add lemon rind and extract. Sift together flour, salt and baking powder. Add dry ingredients alternately with milk, beating with mixer at medium speed. Begin and end with dry ingredients. Pour batter into a greased and floured 6½-cup ring mold. Bake in a 325° oven for 30 to 40 minutes. Cool on wire rack for 10 minutes. Loosen edges and invert. Sprinkle with confectioners' sugar. Fill center with strawberries and top with whipped cream. Serves 10 to 12.

Summer

Fruits and Vegetables
June–August

Inexpensive		Affordable
Apricots	Lettuce	Apples
Avocados	Limes	Artichokes
Bananas	Melons	Asparagus
Beans	Nectarines	Broccoli
Beets	Onions	Cauliflower
Blueberries	Peaches	Eggplant
Cabbage	Pears	Grapefruit
Carrots	Pineapples	Mushrooms
Celery	Plums	Oranges
Cherries	Potatoes	Spinach
Corn	Radishes	
Cucumbers	Squash	
Grapes	Strawberries	
Lemons	Tomatoes	

Salads

Gala Fruit-Filled Melon

1 large watermelon
1 cantaloupe
1 pound seedless grapes
3 oranges
1 ripe pineapple
1 quart fresh strawberries, blueberries or other berries in season
¾ cup honey
¼ cup lemon juice
Fresh mint

Lengthwise, cut off top one-third of the watermelon. (Refrigerate this third for future use, wrapped in foil.) Scoop out the fruit from the larger melon section in large pieces and scallop edge of watermelon as shown to form the bowl for holding the fruit. Cut melon balls from the scooped-out fruit and from the cantaloupe. Prepare remaining fruit as for fruit cup, reserving some of the best berries with hulls on for garnish. Combine cut-up fruit in a large bowl and add the honey and lemon juice. (One-half cup kirsch, sherry or apricot brandy may be added if desired.) Chill the melon and the cut-up fruit separately, covered with foil. Fill shell with fruit and garnish with mint leaves.

Greek Salad

¼ cup wine vinegar
  Anchovy oil plus olive oil to make ½ cup
1 bay leaf
1 clove garlic
1 teaspoon oregano
1 head romaine
½ head iceberg lettuce
4 endive leaves
2 red onions, thinly sliced
2 tomatoes, quartered
1 cucumber, scored and sliced
½ green pepper, cut in strips
6 radishes, sliced
8 to 10 Greek olives
1 can anchovy fillets, drained, save oil
¼ to ½ pound feta cheese

Cut garlic in half and spear with toothpick. Combine vinegar, oils, bay leaf, garlic and oregano. Mix well and chill several hours or overnight. Wash and dry greens. Combine with remaining vegetables, anchovy fillets and cheese. Before serving, remove bay leaf and garlic from dressing; shake well and pour over salad. Makes 4 to 6 servings.

Antipasto Salad

2½ cups chick-peas, cooked and drained
2 ounces anchovy fillets, drained
¼ pound (or more) salami, cubed
6 ounces mozzarella cheese, cubed
12 stuffed olives
1 head lettuce, torn in bite-size pieces
4 stalks celery, chopped
1 onion, finely chopped
6 tablespoons vegetable oil (or olive oil)
5 tablespoons wine vinegar
1 teaspoon salt
  Freshly ground black pepper

In a large bowl, combine all ingredients except oil, vinegar, and seasonings. In a covered jar or blender, combine oil, vinegar, salt, and pepper to taste. Blend well and pour over chick-pea mixture. Toss carefully; correct seasonings. Garnish with parsley or chives, as desired. 12 servings.

Note: You can make ahead if you keep lettuce out until the last moment; then add and toss lightly.

Cucumbers in Sour Cream

2 large cucumbers, peeled, and sliced
2 tablespoons sour cream
1½ tablespoons mayonnaise
3 tablespoons chopped fresh dill
or 2 tablespoons dill seed
Freshly ground black pepper to taste

Combine all ingredients in a serving dish. Taste and correct seasonings. Refrigerate at least one hour before serving. Serves 6.

Herb Yogurt Dressing

1 cup plain yogurt
¼ cup parsley, minced
¼ cup mayonnaise
3 green onions, snipped
1 tablespoon lemon juice or vinegar
Salt and pepper to taste
2 teaspoons sugar

Mix all ingredients until well blended. May be used for a green salad or as a sauce for cold meat or fish. Makes 1½ cups.

Vegetables

Deluxe Green Beans

3 cups sliced fresh or frozen green beans
2 tablespoons margarine or butter
⅓ cup chopped onion
2 tablespoons whole wheat flour
½ teaspoon salt
Freshly ground black pepper to taste
1 cup dairy sour cream
½ cup grated Cheddar cheese

Steam beans until tender (about 10 minutes). Preheat oven to 350°. Melt butter in a small, heavy-bottomed pan; add onion and sauté until tender. Stir in flour, salt, and pepper. When thoroughly mixed, add the sour cream very carefully and heat. Do not boil. Taste and correct seasonings. Stir sour cream mixture into hot beans; pour beans into a greased 1-quart casserole. Top with cheese. Bake about 15 minutes or until cheese melts and beans are heated. 8 servings.

Vegetables Vinaigrette

⅔ cup salad oil
⅓ cup tarragon vinegar
1 teaspoon sugar
1 teaspoon salt
¼ teaspoon Tabasco
1 tablespoon dill weed
2 tablespoons snipped parsley
1 tablespoon snipped chives
½ pound fresh mushrooms, sliced
2 cups raw cauliflower buds
1 can artichoke hearts, drained
1 1-pound can whole green beans, drained

Combine salad oil, vinegar, sugar, salt, Tabasco, dill, parsley and chives and mix until thoroughly blended. Pour over vegetables and marinate in the refrigerator at least 3 hours before serving. This vegetable dish improves with age and will keep for several days in the refrigerator. Serves 12.

Desserts

Peach Kuchen with Streusel Topping

Crust

1¼ cups flour
1 teaspoon baking powder
1 tablespoon sugar
¼ pound butter
1 egg, slightly beaten
1 tablespoon milk

Mix first 3 ingredients together, then add butter and mix or cut in as for piecrust. Mix together egg and milk and add to above. Press in sides and bottom of 9 x 13-inch pan.

Filling

4 to 6 peaches, peeled and halved
1 egg, slightly beaten
1 cup sour cream
1½ tablespoons flour
¾ cup sugar

Place peaches on crust, cut side up. Mix egg, sour cream, flour and sugar. Pour over fruit.

Streusel Topping

¾ cup sugar
2 tablespoons butter, softened
2 tablespoons flour
½ teaspoon cinnamon

Cream sugar and butter; cut in flour and cinnamon. Cover fruit with streusel and bake at 350° for 45 minutes or until fruit is baked and streusel is a delicate brown.

Blitz Torte

4 eggs, separated
1½ cups sugar
½ cup butter, softened
¼ cup milk
½ cup flour
1 teaspoon baking powder
2 teaspoons vanilla
½ cup chopped nuts
½ cup heavy cream, whipped
1 pint fresh sliced strawberries

Cream ½ cup of the sugar with the butter. Blend in beaten egg yolks; then add milk and flour alternately. Add baking powder and vanilla. Place mixture in two greased 8-inch cake pans. In a separate bowl beat egg whites until stiff, gradually adding the remaining sugar. Fold in nuts. Spread half of the meringue over each layer. Bake at 375° for 25 minutes. Cool in pans on wire racks. Place one layer on serving plate, meringue side up and cover with strawberries followed by whipped cream. Follow this procedure for the second layer.

Sour Cherry Cake with Frosting

1¼ cups sugar
½ cup softened butter
¾ cup sour milk
2 eggs
2 cups all-purpose flour
1 teaspoon baking soda
¼ teaspoon salt
1 teaspoon cinnamon
1 cup sour cherries

Grease two 8-inch pans and dust with flour. Cream butter and sugar. Beat in eggs, one at a time. In a separate bowl sift flour, soda, salt and cinnamon. Add butter mixture to flour mixture alternately with milk, beating after each addition. Fold in cherries. Bake in 350° oven for 30 minutes or until done.

Sour Cherry Frosting

1 tablespoon softened butter
1 tablespoon shortening
2½ cups confectioners' sugar
1 teaspoon vanilla
¼ cup sour cherries

Make cherry juice by cooking cherries in a small amount of water and sugar to form a syrup. Strain.

Mix all ingredients with enough cherry juice to obtain a spreadable consistency.

Peach Pudding

3 to 4 medium peaches, sliced
¾ cup sugar
1 egg
2 tablespoons shortening
½ cup milk
1 cup flour
Pinch of salt
1 teaspoon baking powder
1 teaspoon vanilla

Butter a 9-inch glass pie plate. Fill with sliced peaches. Combine remaining ingredients and pour over peaches. Bake at 350° for 30 minutes or until cake tester inserted in center of pudding comes out clean.

Blueberry Cake with Cinnamon Topping

¼ pound butter, softened
¾ cup sugar
1 egg
½ cup milk
1 teaspoon vanilla
2 cups flour
2 teaspoons baking powder
½ teaspoon salt
1 pint blueberries

Cream butter and sugar until soft. Beat in egg. Stir in milk and vanilla until blended. Stir in flour, salt and baking powder. Fold in blueberries. Spoon into a greased 9 x 9-inch cake pan.

Cinnamon Topping

½ cup sugar
⅛ stick butter or margarine
½ teaspoon cinnamon

Lightly mix all ingredients together with a fork until crumbly. Sprinkle on top of cake batter. Bake at 350° for 50 minutes.

Daiquiri Pie

1 9-inch graham cracker crust
1 8-ounce package cream cheese, softened
1 14-ounce can sweetened condensed milk
1 6-ounce can frozen limeade concentrate, thawed
⅓ cup light rum
Green food coloring
1 4½-ounce container frozen whipped topping, thawed Lime slices

Beat cream cheese until light and fluffy. Add milk and limeade, beating smooth. Add rum and food coloring; fold in whipped cream. Pour into pie shell and refrigerate 6 to 8 hours. Garnish with slices of lime, if desired.

Fall

Fruits and Vegetables
September-November

Inexpensive		Affordable
Apples	Grapes	Artichokes
Bananas	Lemons	Avocados
Beets	Lettuce	Beans
Broccoli	Onions	Cantaloupes
Brussels Sprouts	Oranges	Corn
Cabbage	Pears	Grapefruit
Carrots	Peppers	Honeydews
Cauliflower	Potatoes	Limes
Celery	Radishes	Mushrooms
Cranberries	Rutabagas	Pineapples
Cucumbers	Squash	Plums
Eggplant	Tomatoes	Spinach

Salads

Grapefruit Ring

    2   3-ounce packages lemon gelatin
    1½ cups boiling water
    1¾ cups cold water
    ½   cup frozen lemonade concentrate
    2   grapefruits, pared and sectioned (2 cups
        segments)
    1   cup red grapes, halved and seeded
    ½   cup slivered almonds (optional)

Dissolve gelatin in boiling water. Stir in cold water and lemonade. Chill until mixture is partially set. Fold in grapefruit segments, grapes and almonds. Spoon into a 6-cup mold. Chill until firm. Serves 8.

Deli Cole Slaw

    3   pounds cabbage, shredded
    2   onions, chopped
    1   green pepper chopped or sliced
    1   cup vinegar
    1   cup safflower oil
    1   tablespoon celery seed
    1   teaspoon salt
    1   cup sugar

In a saucepan, combine vinegar, oil, celery seed and salt; bring to a boil. Stir in sugar. Combine cabbage, onion and green pepper in a bowl. Pour dressing over and refrigerate up to 3 weeks if necessary. Serves 8 to 10.

Mom's Carrot and Raisin Salad

    3   cups grated raw carrots
    1   cup seedless raisins
    1   tablespoon honey
    6   tablespoons mayonnaise
    ¼   cup milk
    1   tablespoon fresh lemon juice
    ¼   teaspoon salt

Toss carrots and raisins together. Blend remaining ingredients and pour over carrots and raisins. Stir carefully and thoroughly. Chill to blend flavors.

Easy Tomato Aspic

    1   cup water
    1   3-ounce package lemon gelatin
    1   16-ounce can tomatoes
    1   tablespoon vinegar
    1   tablespoon sugar

Dissolve gelatin in boiling water. Cut canned tomatoes into smaller pieces and heat. Stir gelatin, vinegar, and sugar into tomatoes. Pour into a 6" x 9" oiled pan. Refrigerate over night. Serve in squares with salad dressing.

German-Style Potato Salad

    5   pounds potatoes
    6   slices bacon, diced
    4   tablespoons flour
    4   cups water
    6   tablespoons sugar
    1   teaspoon salt
    ⅛   teaspoon pepper
    1   teaspoon (heaping) celery salt
    ¾   cup vinegar
    ½   cup onion, chopped
    6   hard-cooked eggs, sliced

Boil potatoes in their skins in salted water until tender. Peel while still warm. Cool. Slice into a large bowl. Fry bacon until crisp. Remove and drain. Stir flour into bacon fat and blend with a wooden spoon. Add water gradually, stirring until smooth and thick. Add sugar, salt, pepper and celery salt. Simmer and stir until dissolved. Add vinegar and bring to a boil. Pour over the sliced potatoes, add onion and sliced eggs. Refrigerate. Serves 12.

Tomato Aspic
Garden Harvest Casserole p. 16
Mother's Old-Fashioned Apple Pie p. 17

Vegetables
Potato Casserole

6 tablespoons butter
6 Idaho potatoes, peeled and thinly sliced
1¼ cups grated Parmesan cheese
¼ teaspoon nutmeg
½ cup grated Swiss cheese
¼ cup cream
2 tablespoons chopped chives
Salt and pepper to taste

Preheat oven to 400°. Mix together the Parmesan cheese, salt, pepper and nutmeg. Layer potatoes in buttered 2-quart casserole, sprinkling each layer with the Parmesan cheese mixture. Cover tightly and bake at 400° for 1 hour. Uncover, pour cream on top and sprinkle with grated Swiss cheese. Continue to bake, uncovered, for 5 minutes or until cheese is melted. Sprinkle top with chives before serving. Serves 6.

Garden Harvest Casserole

1 cup sliced and unpeeled eggplant
1 cup thinly sliced carrots
1 cup sliced green beans
1 cup diced potatoes
2 medium tomatoes, quartered
1 small yellow squash, sliced
1 small zucchini, sliced
1 medium onion, sliced
½ cup chopped green pepper
½ cup chopped cabbage
3 cloves garlic, crushed
3 sprigs parsley, chopped
Freshly ground black pepper
1 cup beef bouillon
⅓ cup vegetable oil
2 teaspoons salt
¼ teaspoon tarragon
½ bay leaf, crumpled

Mix vegetables and garlic together and place into a shallow baking dish (13 x 9 x 2 inch). Sprinkle parsley and grind pepper over all. At this point you can refrigerate until ready to bake. Preheat oven to 350°. Pour bouillon into a small saucepan; add oil, salt, tarragon, and bay leaf. Heat to boiling; correct seasonings. Pour over vegetables. Cover baking dish with aluminum foil; bake 1 to 1½ hours or until vegetables are just tender and are still colorful. Carefully stir vegetables occasionally, but, to preserve color, don't lift cover off for long. 6-8 servings. servings.

Note: You can substitute other vegetables if they are in harvest and appeal to you.

Zucchini Florentine

3 5-inch zucchini, scrubbed and halved lengthwise
2 tablespoons minced onion
2 packages frozen chopped spinach, thawed
¼ cup grated Parmesan cheese
3 tablespoons butter

Prepare zucchini by scooping out pulp leaving ¼-inch shells; mince pulp. Melt butter in skillet and sauté pulp and onion until tender. Squeeze water out of spinach. Add to zucchini mixture. Makes 6 servings. Keep warm while making sauce.

Sauce

2 tablespoons butter
2 tablespoons flour
1 cup cold milk
Dash nutmeg
¼ teaspoon salt
¼ teaspoon white pepper
¼ teaspoon sugar

Melt butter in skillet over low heat. Add flour; stir for 3 minutes. Add milk, nutmeg, salt, pepper and sugar. Stir until thickened. Add spinach-onion mixture. Arrange zucchini shells in buttered, shallow, oven-proof dish. Divide filling among the shells. Sprinkle each with 1 tablespoon Parmesan and bake in a preheated 350° oven for 30 minutes.

Vegetable Soup

1 cup scrubbed, chopped carrots
¾ cup chopped celery
1 cup chopped onion
1 cup chopped green pepper (deseeded)
2 tablespoons butter or margarine
¼ cup old-fashioned rolled oats
4 cups chicken stock
1¾ cups milk
½ cup nonfat dry milk
1 cup grated aged Cheddar cheese
Salt, Cayenne pepper
Parsley

Place first four vegetables and margarine in a large skillet or Dutch oven and cook, stirring frequently, for 15 minutes or until vegetables are softened and golden. Stir in oats and cook, stirring regularly, for about two minutes. Gradually stir in stock. Bring slowly to a boil and lower heat. Allow mixture to simmer, covered, about 15 minutes. Add milks and stir until smooth (do not boil). Add cheese and seasonings. Heat through. Serve hot, garnished with parsley. 6 servings.

Desserts

Pastry for Two-Crust Pie

1½ cups flour
½ cup shortening
½ teaspoon salt
¼ cup water

Combine flour and salt. Cut in shortening until mixture resembles grains of rice. Add water, a little at a time, mixing to a workable dough. Use more water if needed. Divide dough in half; roll out top and bottom of crust on a floured board.

Mother's Old-Fashioned Apple Pie

4 to 5 cups peeled and sliced tart apples
1½ cups sugar
⅓ cup flour
1 teaspoon cinnamon
¼ cup water
1 tablespoon butter
Pastry for double-crust, 9-inch pie
Milk

Prepare pastry. Roll out half and line pan. Combine sugar, flour and cinnamon in a bowl; stir in water. Add apples, mixing to coat thoroughly. Pour into pan and dot with butter. Roll out top crust; cut a design in the center to allow steam to escape. Place top crust on pie, pressing around the edge to seal. Brush pastry with milk and sprinkle with sugar. Bake in a 350° oven 45 to 60 minutes until crust is browned.

Plum Coffee Cake

¾ cup sugar
½ cup margarine or butter
1 egg
1 teaspoon vanilla
1¼ cups flour
2 teaspoons baking powder
½ teaspoon salt
½ cup milk
6 to 8 fresh Italian plums, pitted and sliced
½ cup brown sugar, firmly packed
3 tablespoons flour
½ teaspoon cinnamon
3 tablespoons melted margarine
¼ cup chopped nuts

Cream together sugar, butter, egg and vanilla. Sift together flour, baking powder and salt. Alternately add milk and dry ingredients to butter mixture. Spread dough in a 9-inch square pan. Top with rows of plum slices. Combine remaining ingredients until crumbly (not smooth) and sprinkle over plums. Bake in a preheated 375° oven for 35 minutes or until done. Cut into squares.

Pumpkin Cheese Pie with Sour Cream Topping

1¼ cups cinnamon-graham cracker crumbs
2 tablespoons sugar
1 teaspoon cinnamon
¼ cup melted butter
1 8-ounce package cream cheese
¾ cup sugar
2 tablespoons flour
1 teaspoon cinnamon
¼ teaspoon nutmeg
¼ teaspoon ginger
1 teaspoon grated lemon peel
1 teaspoon grated orange peel
¼ teaspoon vanilla
1 16-ounce can pumpkin
3 eggs
Salted pecans

Combine graham crumbs, sugar, cinnamon and butter. Mix thoroughly. Press mixture firmly into bottom and up the sides of a 9-inch pie plate. Bake in a 350° oven 10 minutes. Cool. In a large mixing bowl, blend cream cheese, sugar and flour. Add remaining ingredients and beat until smooth. Pour into crust. Cover the edge with a strip of foil to prevent excessive browning. Bake in a 350° oven 50 to 55 minutes or until a knife inserted in the center comes out clean. Remove foil after 35 minutes of baking. At the end of baking time immediately spread on topping. Refrigerate at least 4 hours. Garnish with salted pecans. Serves 8.

Sour Cream Topping

¾ cup sour cream
1 tablespoon sugar
¼ teaspoon vanilla

Combine all ingredients, mixing well.

Pear Clafouti

2 tablespoons sugar
3 cups sliced pears
2 cups milk
3 eggs
¼ cup flour
Pinch salt
3 tablespoons sugar
1 teaspoon vanilla
Confectioners' or brown sugar

Sprinkle a deep dish pie or quiche pan with 2 tablespoons sugar. Place pears on top. In blender beat milk, eggs, flour, salt, 3 tablespoons sugar and vanilla. Blend for 2 minutes. Pour over fruit. Bake in a preheated 375° oven for 45 to 50 minutes until puffed and golden. Sprinkle with confectioners' or brown sugar and glaze under the broiler for a few seconds.

Winter

Fruits and Vegetables
December-February

Inexpensive

Apples	Oranges	
Bananas	Peppers	
Broccoli	Potatoes	
Brussels Sprouts	Radishes	
Cabbages	Rutabagas	
Carrots	Spinach	
Celery	Squash	
Cucumbers	Tomatoes	
Grapefruit		
Lemons		
Lettuce		
Onions		

Affordable

Artichokes
Avocados
Beans
Beets
Cauliflower
Cranberries
Eggplant
Limes
Mushrooms
Pears
Pineapples
Tangerines

Salads

Orange-Avocado Salad

1 avocado, sliced
2 oranges, peeled and sectioned
¼ cup diced red onion
Red-tipped leaf lettuce

Arrange avocado and orange slices on lettuce. Sprinkle with onion. Serve with a clear dressing such as Italian. Serves 4.

Calico Relish

2 cups sliced cauliflower flowerets (about ½ small head)
2 carrots, julienne strips
1 green pepper, cut in strips
10 to 12 green beans
1 zucchini, cut in disks
1 small jar stuffed olives
¾ cup wine vinegar
¼ cup olive oil
1 tablespoon sugar
1 teaspoon salt
½ teaspoon oregano
¼ teaspoon pepper
¼ cup water
Cherry tomatoes (optional)

Combine all ingredients except tomatoes in a large pan. Bring to a boil and simmer, covered, 5 minutes. Cool and let marinate at least 24 hours. Cherry tomatoes may be added just before serving. Makes 2½ quarts.

Cranberry Mold

1 6-ounce package lemon gelatin
2 cups boiling water
1 cup sugar
2 apples, peeled and cored
2 oranges, peeled and sectioned
1 pound fresh cranberries, chopped
3 ounces canned crushed pineapple, drained

Dissolve gelatin in water with 1 cup of sugar. Refrigerate. When gelatin starts to congeal, add chopped apples, oranges, cranberries, and pineapple. Place in 6-cup ring mold and refrigerate until set.

Seven-Layer Salad

1 head iceberg lettuce, shredded
1 green pepper, diced
1 cup chopped celery
1 large onion, chopped
1 16-ounce can peas, drained
2 cups mayonnaise
2 tablespoons brown sugar
½ cup shredded Cheddar cheese
½ cup crisp bacon bits

Prepare salad in a large bowl. Add ingredients one at a time as given, each in a separate layer. Do not toss. Cover and refrigerate for 8 hours or overnight. Serve in bowl, making sure each guest digs down deep to get a portion of each layer. You may also prepare in individual salad bowls, again making seven layers. This salad will keep one or two days if necessary. Makes 8 generous servings.

Vegetables

Rutabaga

3 cups peeled, cubed rutabaga
2 tablespoons butter or margarine
1 tablespoon light brown sugar
2 tablespoons soy sauce
1 tablespoon lemon juice
1 teaspoon Worcestershire sauce

Cook rutabaga in small amount of boiling water or steamer until tender crisp. Combine remaining ingredients; pour over drained rutabaga. Simmer until sauce is reduced and vegetables are glazed. Makes 4 servings.

Seven-Layer Salad
Rutabaga
Moist Cranberry-Apple Cookies p. 21

Saute de Chou

1 medium head cabbage
½ cup butter
4 tablespoons sour cream
Salt and pepper

Wash and finely grate cabbage. Melt butter over high heat. Add cabbage and sauté for 1½ to 2 minutes, stirring constantly, until cabbage is heated through but not wilted. Season with salt and lots of pepper. Stir in sour cream. Serves 4.

Noodle Kugel

2½ cups milk
1 cup butter
1 8-ounce package cream cheese
¾ pound egg noodles
6 eggs
1½ teaspoons salt
Raisins, 2 tablespoons sugar, chopped apple, pineapple tidbits (optional)

Heat milk, butter and cheese thoroughly. Cool. Boil noodles according to package directions; drain. Lightly mix eggs, salt, and optional ingredients into cooled milk mixture and combine with noodles. Pour into a greased 11 x 13-inch oven-proof baking dish and bake in a preheated 325° oven for 45 to 60 minutes until golden brown. Makes 12 servings.

Barley Pilaf Mold

2 cups quick barley
4 cups water with 2 teaspoons instant chicken bouillon
2 ribs celery, chopped
½ green pepper, chopped
½ cup chopped green onion
¼ to ½ pound mushrooms, sliced
2 to 3 tablespoons vegetable oil
3 eggs, slightly beaten
1 cup sour cream
1 teaspoon salt
½ teaspoon white pepper

Stir barley into 4 cups boiling bouillon. Cover and simmer 15 to 20 minutes until tender, stirring occasionally. Drain. Sauté onion, celery, green pepper and mushrooms in oil for a few minutes. Combine sour cream, eggs, salt, pepper and barley. Stir in vegetables. Spoon into a heavily greased 4-cup mold. Chill. Set mold in pan filled with 1½ inches of boiling water. Bake in a 375° oven for 1 hour. Allow to cool 5 minutes. Turn out on platter. Serves 10 to 12.

Potatoes Savoyard

2½ pounds potatoes, peeled, thinly sliced
6 tablespoons butter
2 tablespoons snipped parsley
1 cup grated Swiss cheese (¼ pound)
1 teaspoon salt
⅛ teaspoon freshly ground pepper
1¼ cups boiling beef broth

Preheat oven to 425°. With 2 tablespoons of butter, grease a shallow 2-quart baking dish. Dry potatoes well; use half of them to line the dish, overlapping them. Dot with 2 tablespoons butter, half the parsley, salt, pepper and cheese. Add second layer of potatoes, again overlapping them, and sprinkle with remaining parsley, salt, pepper, cheese; dot with 2 tablespoons butter. Pour boiling broth over and bake in a 425° oven, 55 to 60 minutes until potatoes are fork tender, tops are browned and broth has been absorbed. Serves 6 to 8.

Desserts

Carrot Cake with Cream Cheese Icing

2 cups sugar
2 cups flour
2 teaspoons baking soda
1 teaspoon salt
3 teaspoons cinnamon
1½ cups vegetable oil
4 eggs
3 cups grated carrots
1 cup chopped nuts (optional)
1 teaspoon vanilla

Sift together sugar, flour, soda, salt and cinnamon. Stir in oil. Add eggs, one at a time, mixing well after each addition. Add carrots, nuts and vanilla, mixing thoroughly. Pour into a floured and greased 13 x 9 x 2-inch cake pan. Bake in a 350° oven for 30 minutes. Cool in pan. Spread with Cream Cheese Icing.

Cream Cheese Icing

½ cup melted butter
1 8-ounce package cream cheese, softened
1 teaspoon vanilla
1 1-pound box confectioners' sugar

Combine butter, cream cheese and vanilla, mixing well. Gradually add confectioners' sugar, beating until smooth. Spread on cooled cake.

Pots de Creme

1 6-ounce pkg. semisweet chocolate chips
1¼ cups light cream
2 egg yolks, beaten until thick with a dash of salt

In a heavy dry saucepan, over very low heat, stir chocolate until nearly melted. Stir in light cream and stir until smooth. Gradually stir egg yolks into chocolate mixture. Spoon into pots de creme cups or small glasses, filling two-thirds full. Cover and chill at least 3 hours.

Variation: For Mocha Pots de Creme add: ¼ cup sugar, 1 tablespoon instant coffee and ¼ cup coffee-flavored liqueur to cream.

Old-Fashioned Rice Pudding

2 large eggs
½ cup sugar
½ teaspoon salt
2 cups milk
2 cups cooked rice
½ cup seedless raisins
½ cup chopped cooking apples
1 teaspoon vanilla
Dash nutmeg

Blend together eggs, sugar and salt. Scald milk. Slowly stir in egg mixture. Blend. Add rice, raisins, apples and vanilla. Mix well. Pour into a 3-quart casserole. Sprinkle top with nutmeg. Set casserole in a pan of water and bake in a 350° oven for 1 hour and 15 minutes. Bake until knife inserted into pudding comes out clean. Serve warm with cream or milk. Makes 6 servings.

Gingerbread

1½ cups flour
½ teaspoon baking powder
½ teaspoon baking soda
1 teaspoon salt
1½ teaspoons ginger
¾ teaspoon cinnamon
⅓ cup salad oil
½ cup brown sugar, firmly packed
1 egg, well-beaten
½ cup molasses
½ cup boiling water

Sift together first six ingredients. Make a well and add first the oil, then brown sugar and egg. Mix molasses and boiling water and add to batter. Beat until smooth. Turn into a greased 8-inch square pan. Bake in a 350° oven 35 to 40 minutes. Makes 6 to 8 servings.

Moist Cranberry-Apple Cookies

½ cup butter or margarine
1 cup brown sugar
¾ cup sugar
1 egg
¼ cup milk
2 cups flour
1 teaspoon baking powder
1 teaspoon cinnamon
½ teaspoon salt
1 teaspoon grated orange rind
1½ cups pared apples, chopped
1 cup cranberries, chopped

Cream butter and sugars; beat in egg and milk. Sift together flour, baking powder, cinnamon and salt. Stir into butter mixture until well blended. Stir in orange rind, apple and cranberries. Drop by teaspoons onto greased cookie sheets. Bake at 375° for 12 to 15 minutes. Makes about 4 dozen cookies.

Chocolate Thumbprints

1 1-ounce square unsweetened chocolate
½ cup butter or margarine
½ cup sugar
1 egg, separated
¼ teaspoon vanilla
1 cup flour
¼ teaspoon salt
¾ cup finely chopped nuts
1 6-ounce package semisweet chocolate chips

Melt chocolate over hot, not boiling, water. Cool slightly. Cream butter; add melted chocolate. Add sugar, egg yolk and vanilla and mix thoroughly. Sift together flour and salt. Add to chocolate mixture. Slightly beat egg white with fork. Roll dough into balls (about 1 teaspoon per ball), and dip balls in egg white to coat. Roll in nuts. Place about 1 inch apart on ungreased cookie sheet; press thumb gently in center of each. Bake in preheated 350° oven 10 to 12 minutes or until set. Transfer to cake rack. Immediately place 3 or 4 chocolate chips in the "thumbprint." When the chips have melted, spread evenly over the thumbprint. Makes about 3 dozen cookies.

Here's a week of low cost dinners to please any budget or appetite. The mainstays of each night's dinner are inexpensive ingredients used creatively. We've prepared a delicious Roast Turkey with Stuffing for Sunday . . . this versatile dish need not be relegated to Thanksgiving. Leftovers are shown off in Creamed Turkey on Tuesday. Monday night's fare is Eggplant Parmigiana. Wednesday features Bean Tostada for a Mexican change of pace. Thursday recreates one of Grandma's favorites, Chicken Stew with Carrot Dumplings. Friday takes a visit to the eastern seaboard with Manhattan Chowder. Chicken del Prado provides a splendid repast for Saturday night's company dinner.

Sunday

Roast Turkey

To Thaw: Place turkey in original bag on tray in refrigerator. Allow 2 days for 8- to 11-pound bird; 2 to 3 days for 11- to 14-pound bird; 3 to 4 days for 14- to 24-pound bird. Refreezing is not recommended.

To Prepare: Free legs and tail from tucked position; remove neck from body cavity and giblets from neck cavity. Rinse and drain turkey. If desired, stuff neck and body cavities lightly, allowing ¾ cup stuffing per pound weight of uncooked turkey. Return tail and legs to tucked position. Skewer neck skin to back. Insert meat thermometer into center of thigh, next to body but not touching bone. Place turkey, breast side up, on rack in shallow, open pan. Do not add water or cover. Use following time chart.

Approximate Roasting Time

Weight as Purchased	325° Oven
8 to 12 lbs.	3½ to 4 hours
12 to 16 lbs.	4 to 4½ hours
16 to 20 lbs.	4½ to 5 hours
20 to 24 lbs.	5 to 6 hours

Brush skin with melted butter to prevent drying. Baste frequently during roasting unless using a pre-basted turkey. When light golden brown, shield breast and neck with lightweight aluminum foil to prevent over-browning. During last hour of cooking check for doneness.

To Test for Doneness: Before removing from oven, check to be sure meat thermometer is in original position. Thigh temperature should be 180° to 185°. Protect fingers with paper. Press thigh and drumstick. Meat should feel soft. Prick skin at thigh. Juices should no longer be pink.

Basic Stuffing

> 8 cups soft bread crumbs
> ½ cup butter or sausage drippings
> 1 large onion, grated
> 1½ teaspoons salt
> ¼ teaspoon pepper
> Seasonings as suggested

Tear or grate bread. (If using crusts, cut into fine shreds.) Mix together crumbs and soft butter, onion, salt and pepper. Add desired seasonings. Toss together lightly. 9 cups.

Note: A 1-pound loaf of bread makes about 10 cups of bread crumbs.

Pork Sausage Stuffing

> ½ pound pork sausage
> Basic Stuffing

Brown sausage over medium heat, breaking apart with fork. Use sausage drippings in Basic Stuffing. Add sausage to Basic Stuffing and mix well.

Savory Stuffing

> ¾ teaspoon thyme
> ¾ teaspoon sweet marjoram
> ¾ teaspoon sage
> Basic Stuffing

Add seasonings to Basic Stuffing; mix well.

Monday

Eggplant Parmigiana

    1   1-pound eggplant
    ¼ cup flour
    ½ teaspoon salt
    1   beaten egg
    ½ cup vegetable oil
    ½ cup grated Parmesan cheese
    2   cups tomato sauce
    1   6-ounce package sliced mozzarella cheese

Peel eggplant and cut into ½-inch slices. Combine flour and salt. Dip eggplant into beaten egg, then into flour mixture. Brown in hot oil in large skillet; drain well on paper towels. Place 1 layer of eggplant in a 10 x 6 x 2-inch baking dish, cutting to fit. Sprinkle with half the Parmesan, half of the tomato sauce, and half of the mozzarella. Cut remaining mozzarella into triangles. Repeat layers, ending with mozzarella on top. Bake, uncovered, in a 400° oven for 20 minutes. Serves 6.

Tomato Sauce

    ⅓ cup chopped onion
    ¼ cup finely chopped celery
    ½ clove of garlic, minced
    1   teaspoon parsley flakes
    2   tablespoons olive oil
    1   16-ounce can Italian tomatoes
    ⅓ cup tomato paste
    ½ teaspoon salt
    ½ teaspoon dried oregano
    ¼ teaspoon pepper
    1   bay leaf

In a small saucepan cook onion, celery, garlic and parsley in hot oil until tender but not brown. Add tomatoes, tomato paste, salt, pepper, oregano and bay leaf. Simmer, gently, uncovered 45 to 50 minutes. Remove bay leaf. May be prepared ahead and refrigerated or frozen until needed. Reheat to serve. Makes 2 cups.

Tuesday

Creamed Turkey

    1   tablespoon butter
    3   tablespoons minced onion
    1   tablespoon chopped parsley
    2   cups leftover turkey, diced
    2   cups frozen peas
    2   tablespoons leftover turkey gravy
        Pinch nutmeg
        Salt and pepper to taste

Melt butter in a skillet and lightly sauté onion and parsley. Stir in turkey, peas, gravy, nutmeg, salt and pepper. Keep warm while preparing the following cream sauce.

Add turkey mixture to cream sauce and blend well. Serve at once over hot, fluffy rice, buttered noodles or hot corn bread, split and generously buttered. Serves 5 to 6.

Cream Sauce

    1½ tablespoons butter
    1½ tablespoons flour
    1½ cups top milk or ¾ cup each milk and cream
    2   eggs, beaten

Combine butter, flour and milk in saucepan. Cook, stirring constantly, until smooth and thickened. Season to taste. Quickly stir in eggs.

Wednesday

Bean Tostada

    4   cups water or vegetable cooking liquid
    2   cups dry pinto beans
    2   cups chopped onion
    2   garlic cloves, minced
    1   yellow hot pepper or 2 small green, chopped
    ½ teaspoon crushed hot red peppers (dry)
    ½ teaspoon sweet red pepper flakes
    4   tablespoons fresh oregano or 2 tablespoons dried
    1   tablespoon ground coriander seed
    1   tablespoon cumin seed
    1   teaspoon paprika
    ⅛ teaspoon cayenne pepper
    4   large ripe tomatoes, chopped or 2 cups canned tomato
        Dash of freshly ground black pepper
    1½ teaspoon salt
    6   stone ground corn tortillas

Bring water to boil; add beans, cover and cook for two minutes. Turn off heat and let stand for two hours. Add remaining ingredients except salt and tortillas. Simmer 2 to 3 hours or until beans are tender. Add salt the last 15 to 20 minutes. Taste and correct seasonings. Just before serving, heat tortillas in oven or sauté briefly in a small amount of oil and drain on paper towels. Keep warm until ready to serve. Spoon bean mixture on top of tortillas. Garnish with shredded lettuce, chopped tomatoes, grated Cheddar or Monterey Jack cheese or yogurt. Serves 6.

Note: May be used as pita filling or on whole wheat bread or toast.

Thursday

Chicken Stew with Carrot Dumplings

> 1 stewing chicken, cut up
> 1 medium onion, sliced
> 1 stalk celery, sliced
> 2 teaspoons salt
> 1/8 teaspoon thyme
> 1/8 teaspoon pepper
> 3 tablespoons flour
> 1/3 cup water
>   Carrot dumplings

Put chicken, onion, celery, seasonings and water to cover in a large kettle or Dutch oven. Bring to a boil. Cover. Reduce heat and simmer for 2½ to 3 hours or until chicken is tender. With slotted spoon remove chicken. Cool enough to remove bones from meat. Skim fat from broth. Blend in flour mixed with water and stir over medium heat until slightly thickened. Add chicken meat. Bring to a boil. Drop in dumplings. Cover and simmer for 15 minutes. Serves 8.

Carrot Dumplings

> 1 cup flour
> 2 teaspoons baking powder
> 1/2 teaspoon salt
> 3 tablespoons shortening
> 1/2 cup milk
> 1/4 cup shredded carrot
> 1 teaspoon parsley flakes

Sift together flour, baking powder, and salt. Cut in shortening. Add in milk, carrot and parsley, stirring until flour is moist. Drop dumplings into simmering liquid in 8 mounds. Cover. Simmer 15 minutes without lifting cover. Serves 8.

Friday

Manhattan Chowder

> 1 4½-ounce can clams
> 1 pound fish fillet
> 1/2 cup chopped bacon
> 1/4 cup chopped onion
> 1/4 cup green pepper, chopped
> 1 cup celery, chopped
> 1 cup potatoes, diced
> 1/4 teaspoon thyme
> 1 teaspoon salt
>   Dash of cayenne pepper
> 2 cups tomato juice

Drain clams, reserving liquid. Add enough water to make 1 cup. Chop clams. Cut fish into ½-inch cubes. Fry bacon until lightly browned. Add onions, green pepper and celery. Cook until tender. Add liquid from clams. Add potatoes and seasonings to bacon and onion mixture. Add fish and clams. Cook for 15 minutes or until potatoes are tender. Add tomato juice and heat. Serves 6.

Saturday

Chicken Del Prado

> 2 fryers, cut up
> 1/2 cup flour
> 1½ teaspoons salt
> 1/2 teaspoon pepper
> 1/2 cup vegetable oil
> 2 cloves garlic, minced
> 1 large onion, diced
> 2 ribs celery, sliced
> 1 green pepper, cut in strips
> 1/2 pound mushrooms, sliced
> 1 teaspoon crushed thyme
> 1/4 teaspoon cayenne pepper
> 1 bay leaf
> 1 14-ounce can Italian plum tomatoes
> 1 cup dry white wine
> 2 tablespoons tomato paste
> 8 to 10-ounce cooked, drained spaghetti

Combine flour, salt and pepper and dust chicken. Save any flour mixture that is leftover. Brown chicken, a few pieces at a time in oil in a large skillet. Place browned chicken in large casserole. In same skillet with no more than 2 tablespoons of leftover oil, sauté garlic, onion, celery, green pepper and mushrooms until just tender and crisp. Add leftover flour mixture, thyme, cayenne and bay leaf. Stir to coat vegetables. Add plum tomatoes and liquid, wine and tomato paste. Stir to blend. Bring to a boil and pour over chicken in casserole. Cover and bake in a 350° oven for 60 minutes or until chicken is tender. Serve with bowl of buttered spaghetti. Serves 6 to 8.

Here's a delicious variety of meals in a dish. All are hearty courses and can be easily complemented with the addition of a crisp salad and a quick bread. All of these dishes enhance the flavor and tenderness of inexpensive cuts of meat. Seasonal produce is also utilized in many of these featured recipes to stretch your budget.

Southern Gumbo

¼ cup bacon drippings or butter
1 large onion, chopped
2 cups canned tomatoes
1½ teaspoon salt
½ teaspoon pepper
3 cups okra, sliced
3 cups chicken bouillon
1 cup uncooked rice

Melt drippings or butter in large heavy soup kettle. Add onion. Sauté until lightly browned. Add remaining ingredients. Tightly cover. Heat to boiling, then reduce heat. Simmer for 30 minutes. Serve hot. Serves 6.

Speedy Spinach Lasagne

1 package spaghetti sauce mix
1 6-ounce can tomato paste
1 8-ounce can tomato sauce
1¾ cups cold water
2 eggs
1 15-ounce container ricotta or 1 pound creamed cottage cheese
½ teaspoon salt
1 10-ounce package frozen chopped spinach, thawed and drained
½ cup grated Parmesan cheese
½ pound sliced mozzarella cheese
½ pound uncooked lasagne noodles, broken in half

Empty spaghetti sauce mix into saucepan; add tomato paste, tomato sauce and water. Heat, stirring, until well blended. Remove from heat. Beat eggs in a large bowl and add Ricotta or cottage cheese, spinach, salt and ¼ cup Parmesan cheese. Lightly grease bottom of a 13 x 9 x 2-inch baking dish; cover with a little sauce. Layer noodles, half of the cheese-spinach mixture, half the mozzarella cheese and half the tomato sauce. Repeat layers. Sprinkle with ¼ cup Parmesan cheese. Cover dish with a lightly greased sheet of aluminum foil and bake in a preheated 350° oven for 60 minutes or until noodles are tender. Let stand 10 minutes before cutting in squares and serving. Serves 8.

Egg Casserole

¼ cup butter
¼ cup flour
2½ cups milk
¼ teaspoon thyme
¼ teaspoon marjoram
1 pound grated Cheddar cheese
2 dozen hard-boiled eggs, sliced
1 pound bacon, fried and crumbled
½ cup snipped parsley

Melt butter; stir in flour. Gradually add in milk, stirring constantly. Add thyme, marjoram and cheese, stirring constantly, until cheese melts. In a large greased casserole, make layers of eggs, bacon, cheese sauce and parsley. Bake in a preheated 350° oven 30 minutes. Serves 8 to 10.

Chicken Paprika Casserole

8 ounce egg noodles
1 small onion, chopped
¼ cup butter
2 chickens, about 2 pounds each, quartered
¼ cup flour
1 teaspoon salt
½ teaspoon pepper
1 tablespoon sweet paprika
2 cups chicken broth
2 tablespoons tomato sauce
2 teaspoons Worcestershire sauce
2 cups sour cream

Cook noodles until barely tender, drain and put in 5-quart casserole. Sauté onion in the butter. Remove onion and, in same skillet, sauté chicken a few pieces at a time until lightly browned on both sides. Add more butter if necessary. Arrange chicken on noodles. Blend flour into drippings in skillet. Add salt, pepper and paprika. Cook, stirring, 1 or 2 minutes. Add chicken broth and cook until slightly reduced and thickened. Remove from heat, add tomato sauce, Worcestershire sauce and sour cream and pour over chicken. Bake in 350° oven about 1½ hours. Makes 6 to 8 servings.

Madras Beef and Fruit Casserole

2 pounds lean stew beef
3 tablespoons butter or 2 tablespoons salad oil
2 cups water
Juice and rind of 1 lemon
2 cups mixed dried fruit
1 tablespoon cinnamon or 2 teaspoons curry

In a heavy skillet, brown meat in butter or oil. Stir in water, dried fruit, lemon juice and rind, cinnamon or curry. Pour into a covered casserole. Place into a 325° oven for 1½ hours. Serves 4.

Sauerkraut Casserole

2 pounds sauerkraut
½ cup diced smoked sausage
1 large carrot, diced
1 onion, chopped
12 peppercorns
1 cup dry white wine
2 cups diced smoked ham
½ cup diced bacon
1 large apple, diced
1 large potato, pared and grated
1 cup stock or water

Drain sauerkraut. Combine all ingredients and pour in a buttered 2-quart casserole. Cover and bake in a 350° oven for 1½ to 2 hours. Casserole should be fairly dry. Serves 6.

Chicken-Broccoli Casserole

1 3-pound frying chicken
2 10-ounce packages frozen broccoli or 2 bunches fresh broccoli
1 cup mayonnaise
2 10¾-ounce cans condensed cream of chicken soup
¼ teaspoon curry powder
1 tablespoon lemon juice
½ cup grated Cheddar cheese
½ cup bread crumbs
1 tablespoon melted butter

Stew chicken; cool and bone. Steam broccoli until tender; drain. Grease an 11 x 7-inch casserole. Place chicken on the bottom, broccoli on top. Combine mayonnaise, soup, curry powder and lemon juice. Pour over broccoli. Sprinkle with a mixture of cheese and bread crumbs combined with butter. Bake in a 350° oven for 30 minutes. Serves 6.

Patchwork Casserole

2 pounds ground chuck
2 green peppers, chopped
1 large onion, chopped
2 pounds frozen Southern-style hash brown potatoes
2 8-ounce cans tomato sauce
1 6-ounce can tomato paste
1 cup water
1 teaspoon salt
½ teaspoon basil
¼ teaspooon pepper
1 pound processed American cheese, thinly sliced

Brown meat; drain. Add green pepper and onion; cook until tender. Add remaining ingredients except cheese; mix well. Spoon half of meat and potato mixture into 13½ x 8¾-inch baking dish or two 1½-quart casserole dishes. Cover with half the cheese. Top with remaining meat and potato mixture. Cover dish with aluminum foil. Bake in preheated 350° oven 45 minutes. Uncover. Cut remaining cheese into decorative shapes; arrange in patchwork design on casserole. Let stand 5 minutes or until cheese shapes have melted. 12 servings. Can be frozen.

Pork-Noodle Casserole

2 tablespoons butter
2 green onions, cut in ½-inch pieces
1 green pepper, cut in ½-inch pieces
1 stalk celery, cut in ½-inch pieces
1 clove garlic, minced
2 cups chicken broth
¼ cup cornstarch
2 tablespoons soy sauce
1 tablespoon bead molasses
½ teaspoon salt
Dash white pepper
2 tablespoons dry white wine
2 cups diced roast pork
1 16-ounce can fancy Chinese mixed vegetables, rinsed and drained
1 3-ounce can chow mein noodles

Melt butter in saucepan; add green onions, green pepper, celery and garlic. Stir just until heated through. Combine broth, cornstarch, soy sauce, bead molasses, salt and pepper. Cook over low heat until clear and thickened, about 5 minutes; blend in wine. Stir in vegetable mixture, pork and mixed vegetables. Spoon into 4 buttered individual casseroles; line edge with chow mein noodles. Bake in preheated 350° oven 20 minutes or until hot. 4 servings. Can be frozen.

Sausage-Cornbread Pie

    1 pound fresh pork sausage
    1 cup yellow cornmeal
    1 cup flour
    ¼ cup sugar
    4 teaspoons baking powder
    1 egg
    1 cup milk

Brown pork sausage, separating it into pieces. Pour off drippings, reserving ¼ cup. Sift together cornmeal, flour, sugar and baking powder. Add egg, milk and ¼ cup pork sausage drippings. Mix to combine thoroughly. Fold in sausage. Turn batter into a greased 9-inch pie plate. Bake in a 425° oven for 25 minutes or until done. Makes 6 servings.

Chicken Noodle Casserole

    2 2½-pound chickens, cut up
    1 medium onion, quartered
    1 medium carrot, cut up
    1 stalk celery
    3 quarts water
    2 10-ounce packages frozen, chopped spinach
    1 pound broad noodles
    6 tablespoons melted butter
    2 tablespoons butter
    4 tablespoons flour
    1 teaspoon oregano
    1 clove garlic, crushed
    1½ cups white wine
    6 egg yolks
    ½ cup grated Parmesan cheese

In a large pot, combine chicken, carrot, onion, celery and water. Simmer, uncovered, 45 minutes. Skim top. Remove chicken and strain broth. Return broth to pot and boil rapidly until liquid is reduced to about 3 cups. Bone chicken and cut into bite-sized pieces. Cook spinach and noodles separately and drain. Cover bottom of a large, shallow baking pan with noodles mixed with melted butter. Spread chicken pieces on top of noodles. In a small saucepan melt butter and add flour, blending well. Add oregano, garlic and chicken broth and simmer, stirring constantly, until thickened. Fold in spinach and pour mixture over the chicken. If preparing a day ahead, refrigerate at this point. Boil wine until reduced to 1 cup. Beat in egg yolks and cheese and pour over chicken. Bake at 400° for 25 minutes, or until top is golden. Remove from oven and allow to settle for 5 minutes. Serves 8.

Fish and Asparagus Au Gratin

    1 pound fish steaks or fillets, cut in serving
        pieces (trout, whitefish, bass)
    1 tablespoon butter
    ¼ teaspoon salt
    ¼ teaspoon pepper
    1 10-ounce package frozen cut asparagus
    1 10-ounce can Cheddar cheese soup
    ¼ cup milk
    1 cup soft bread crumbs
    2 tablespoons melted butter

Place fish in a greased baking dish; dot with butter and sprinkle with salt and pepper. Bake in a 325° oven for 35 minutes. Meanwhile, cook asparagus as directed on package; drain and place asparagus on top of fish. Combine soup and milk and pour over fish. Combine crumbs and melted butter; sprinkle on top of soup. Return to oven until light brown. Serves 4.

Moussaka

    1 eggplant, peeled and sliced
    1 pound ground lamb or beef
    1 medium onion, chopped
    1 clove garlic, minced
    1 1-pound can tomatoes
    ½ teaspoon oregano
    1 teaspoon salt
    ⅛ teaspoon pepper
    1 tablespoon olive oil
    ½ cup cottage cheese
    2 eggs, slightly beaten
        Nutmeg

Sauté meat, onion and garlic until meat is brown. Drain well. Add tomatoes, oregano, salt, pepper. Simmer 10 minutes. Brush eggplant slices with olive oil and broil for 5 minutes on each side. Make layers of eggplant and meat sauce in a greased casserole. Top with cottage cheese and eggs beaten together. Sprinkle with a little nutmeg. Bake in a preheated 350° oven for 2 hours. Serves 4.

Overnight Casserole

    2 cups macaroni (uncooked)
    ¼ pound shredded cheese
    ¼ pound ground ham
    2 cans cream of mushroom soup
    4 eggs, hard-cooked and diced
    1 onion, minced

Combine above ingredients. Let stand overnight. Bake in a 350° oven 1 hour.

Add Flavor and Lower Cost with Herbs

Herbs ... marvelous bits of flavor to enhance the taste of any food. Each herb is particularly compatible with certain foods, and we've provided a chart to eliminate any guesswork on your part. While herbs can be the perfect compliment to the most expensive cut of veal, they can also work wonders with less expensive cuts of meat and make your budget dish taste like a gourmet entrée! Using herbs will reduce the use of fats and salt in the cooking process, which will increase nutritional benefits at mealtime.

Windowsill Herb Gardens

Their medical properties long since forgotten, herbs were an indispensable part of colonial gardens. And today they are a flavorful added touch, as well as the mainstay of great cuisine.

For those who are ardent admirers and advocates of cooking with herbs, a short passage on growing these delightful plants is provided here to help supply fresh herbs the year round.

As with many houseplants, herbs require moderate attention to their growing needs. A cool, sunny room with temperatures ranging from 50° to 65° is ideal. And while good air circulation is desirable, plants must be protected from sudden drafts or temperature changes.

Provide a rich growing medium and fertilize according to package directions with a 5-10-5 fertilizer. Plants grown indoors can be potted in one part commercial potting soil to which one part peat moss, one part sand and one part bone meal are added.

Use pots that are at least five inches in diameter. Provide adequate drainage by placing broken chards of clay pot over the drainage hole, convex side up, and then adding one inch of gravel before planting.

To plant in window boxes, purchase or construct one that is at least twelve inches wide and twelve inches deep. The length will vary according to the windowsill on which the box will be placed. The box should be filled with at least two inches of gravel for drainage.

Potted plants may be placed directly into the window box and then surrounded by sphagnum moss to help retain moisture.

Water plants in the early morning or late afternoon, while the sun is low, using tepid water. Keep the soil moist, but not wet, and mist often.

The following herbs grow well indoors and are especially valuable in the winter months

Basil

Root cuttings in August. Give proper light and humidity and the plant will grow happily. A tender plant, basil should be carefully harvested to avoid injury to leaves. Can be dried or frozen.

Dill

Dill is an annual which should be sown out-of-doors in a ten-inch pot. Thin seedlings to four or five plants and bring indoors in fall. Freeze snips of green foliage and then mince frozen herbs for use in the dish being prepared.

Marjoram

Select a strong plant from the garden before the first frost. Give plenty of sun and some fertilizer. Dried leaves should be used more sparingly than fresh.

Parsley

A biennial, parsley can be grown from seed planted in late July or early August. If bringing a mature garden plant indoors, choose a small one, since its long taproot requires a tall pot or deep window box. Like most herbs, parsley thrives best on cool but sunny temperatures. Store sprigs in freezer bags and mince as needed.

Rosemary

Bring plant in from the garden. New plants can be started from cuttings. Keeping soil moist and humidity high will enable this plant to flourish indoors. Best when used fresh, rosemary can be dried or the leaves can be frozen.

Savory

Plant seed in early spring directly in the pot in which the plant will be grown. Winter savory is a better houseplant than summer savory. Harvest winter savory by cutting off branch tips before flowering and drying them. Clip summer savory in June or July, and freeze or dry.

Tarragon

Tarragon plants can be purchased from herb growers. This herb needs little or no fertilizer. Cuttings may be frozen in plastic containers and used as needed.

Herbs, clockwise from bottom of picture: garlic, rosemary, chervil, fennel, marjoram, dill, savory, coriander, thyme, sage, basil, and bay leaf.

Drying Herbs

Drying herbs not only preserves most of the natural color, but also stores the volatile oil, which gives them their flavor. Successful drying is achieved with good air circulation and heat in the absence of sunlight and moisture. Herbs should remain undisturbed for ten days to two weeks.

To prepare herbs for drying, first clean the stems and leaves. Then, as soon as all the moisture has evaporated, cut the leaves and/or stems, using a sharp knife or scissors. Handle the leaves very carefully to avoid bruising them. Cut no more than one-third of the growth on perennials. Annuals will withstand greater harvesting.

There are several ways to dry herbs. One method is to tie the herbs into bunches and hang them upside down in a warm, dry place, such as an attic. To catch the dried leaves as they fall and hinder the accumulation of dust, tie a paper bag with an ample number of holes punched in the sides around the herbs.

Another method of drying is to first pick the perfect leaves of the herb, wash them and then spread them on aluminum window screens or frames covered with cheesecloth. Do not crowd the leaves, since those which are not exposed to air will rot and have to be discarded. Place screens or frames in a dry room such as a garage, or an attic.

The herbs will dry in about one week in hot, dry weather, but will take longer in damp, humid weather.

A moderate harvest can be dried by placing herbs on cookie sheets or trays and putting them in a hot oven with a temperature setting of 375°-400°. Leave the door open slightly. Watch the progress carefully and remove as soon as the herbs are crisp.

Air-dried herbs should be tested for dryness by rolling the leaves between your fingers. If they crumble into tiny pieces or powder, they are dry.

Care of Herbs

Please take proper care of your herbs by keeping them tightly covered and in a cool, dry place. Ground herbs will be at their peak flavor up to six months from date of opening, while whole herbs will last for years. These seemingly delicate fragments of leaves should be used sparingly as they can pack a pungent "wallop" if used with abandon.

Savory Combinations

Basil	Fish, shellfish, stews, tomatoes, egg and cheese dishes
Bay leaves	Beef, lamb, veal, fish, stuffings, sauces
Chervil	Beef, lamb, pork, veal, beets, eggplant, spinach, braised lettuce, salads, egg and cheese dishes
Coriander	Ham, fruits, marinades
Dill	Meat loaves, meatballs, shrimp, lobster, salmon, cold vegetable, fish or seafood salads
Fennel	Beef, lamb, pork, chicken, duck, fish, shellfish, salads, fruits, cheese, cakes, cookies, bread, rolls
Garlic	Beef, lamb, pork, stews, chicken, fish, salads, egg dishes, vegetables, breads, dressings, marinades
Marjoram	Beef, lamb, veal roast, stews, meat loaf, meatballs, chicken, duck, turkey, fish, shellfish, salads, egg dishes
Rosemary	Beef, lamb, pork, veal, stews, chicken, turkey, duck, fish, shellfish, egg dishes
Sage	Beef, lamb, pork or veal roasts or stews, chicken, turkey, goose, lima beans, onions, zucchini squash, eggplant, peas, potatoes, tomatoes, Cheddar, cottage and cream cheeses, bread, dressings and marinades.
Savory	Beef, lamb, pork, ham, veal, chicken, eggs, sauces, stuffings, fish, salads
Thyme	Beef, lamb, pork, veal, chicken, fish, snap beans, carrots, eggplant, mushrooms, onions, potatoes, squash, salads, egg and cheese dishes, stuffings

Beef Bourguignon

                    4 slices bacon
                    2 pounds beef chuck or sirloin beef cubes,
                        about 1 inch
                    2 10½-ounce cans condensed beef broth or
                        2½ cups brown stock
                    1 cup Burgundy or other dry red wine
                    2 cloves garlic, minced
                    1 teaspoon salt
                    ⅛ teaspoon pepper
                    ⅛ teaspoon thyme
                    ⅛ teaspoon marjoram
                   10 small onions (about ½ pound)
                    ½ pound sliced fresh mushrooms
                    ⅓ cup water
                    ¼ cup flour
                        Cooked rice or noodles

In Dutch oven or ovenproof pan, cook bacon until crisp. Remove and crumble. Brown meat in drippings; pour off all fat. Add bacon, broth, wine, garlic, salt, pepper, thyme and marjoram. Cover; bake in 350° oven 1 hour and 15 minutes. Add vegetables; bake 1 hour longer or until meat and vegetables are tender. Gradually blend water into flour until smooth; slowly stir into sauce. Cook, stirring until thick. Serve over rice or noodles. 6 servings.

Garlic Herbed Bread Chunks

                    1 large loaf Italian bread
                    ¼ pound butter or margarine
                    ¼ teaspoon oregano
                    ¼ teaspoon paprika
                    1 clove garlic
                    1 teaspoon parsley flakes or 1 tablespoon
                        chopped fresh parsley
                    4 tablespoons grated Parmesan cheese

Cut bread in half lengthwise through the center. Cut bread in thick 2-inch slices, then cut each slice into quarters to make chunks. Have the butter or margarine at room temperature so it is soft. Use a garlic press to crush the garlic, letting the juice run into the butter. Add all the other seasonings and mix together. Spread butter on all sides of bread chunks. Place on a large sheet of foil and secure edges tightly. Refrigerate until shortly before serving. Partially open the foil and heat the bread in the oven for 30 minutes. Remove from foil and serve.

Sauerbraten Steak

                    2½ cups water
                    1 cup wine vinegar
                    1 tablespoon brown sugar
                    1 teaspoon salt
                    6 whole cloves
                    6 peppercorns
                    2 bay leaves
                    2 medium onions, thinly sliced
                    ⅓ cup vegetable oil
                    1 beef blade steak (2½ to 3 pounds), cut
                        1½ inches thick
                    2 tablespoons drippings or cooking fat
                    ¾ cup water
                    ½ cup raisins
                    1 tablespoon brown sugar
                    ⅔ cup crumbled gingersnaps

Combine 2½ cups water, vinegar, 1 tablespoon brown sugar, salt, cloves, peppercorns and bay leaves in saucepan; bring to boil. Pour over sliced onions in bowl; cool. Stir in oil. Pour marinade over steak; refrigerate 8 to 10 hours or overnight, turning at least once. Remove steak from marinade to absorbent paper; pat dry. Heat drippings to 350° in electric frying pan. Brown meat. Pour off drippings. Strain marinade; add 1 cup to steak, reserving remainder. Cover; cook 2 hours or until steak is tender. Remove steak to hot platter and pour off liquid. Add 1½ cups reserved marinade, ¾ cup water, raisins and 1 tablespoon brown sugar to frying pan. Bring to boil. Add crumbled gingersnaps; stir to thicken. Serve gravy with steak. 4 to 6 servings.

Mexican Pot Roast

                    ¾ to 1 pound chuck roast or lean stew beef
                        Vegetable oil
                    1½ cups water
                    1½ teaspoons salt
                    ½ teaspoon sugar
                    ¼ teaspoon pepper
                    1 teaspoon chili powder
                    ⅛ teaspoon ground cumin
                    ⅛ teaspoon dried ground chili peppers
                    1 28-ounce can tomatoes
                    1 large onion, chopped
                    ½ green pepper, chopped
                    1 or 2 carrots, sliced

Brown meat in a little oil. Add water, seasonings and vegetables. Cover and simmer for 1½ to 2 hours. Remove cover; cut meat into bite-size pieces and simmer for an additional 30 minutes until thickened. Serves 4.

Herbed Trout Bake

1 pound fresh or partially thawed frozen trout fillets
¼ cup chopped onion
1 small clove garlic, minced
2 tablespoons butter
½ teaspoon tarragon
¼ teaspoon thyme
¼ teaspoon salt
Dash of pepper
¼ cup cornflake crumbs

Place fillets in greased baking dish. In skillet, sauté onion and garlic in butter until tender; stir in seasonings; simmer 1 minute. Spread onion mixture over fish and top with cornflake crumbs. Bake in a 475° oven 10 to 12 minutes or until fish flakes easily with a fork. Serves 4.

Chicken with Herb Spaghetti

¼ pound butter or margarine, melted
½ cup parsley sprigs
2 cloves garlic, halved
Salt
⅛ teaspoon pepper
1 teaspoon basil leaves
½ teaspoon oregano leaves
2 tablespoons vegetable oil
1 tablespoon lemon juice
2 pounds broiler-fryer chicken pieces
8 ounces spaghetti
3 quarts boiling water
Parsley sprigs

Place butter, parsley, garlic, ½ teaspoon salt, pepper, basil and oregano leaves in blender. Blend at high speed until parsley is finely chopped. (If you do not have a blender, mince parsley and use a garlic press.) Set 3 tablespoons of herb mixture aside for chicken and use the rest to toss with spaghetti. Using a fork, beat together oil and lemon juice. Brush chicken pieces with mixture. Sprinkle with salt and pepper. Broil about 8 inches from heat. Turn chicken after 20 minutes of broiling. Broil an additional 25 minutes. Brush each side of chicken with herb mixture during last 4 minutes of broiling. Prepare spaghetti 15 minutes before chicken is done. Add spaghetti and 1 tablespoon salt to rapidly boiling water. Cook uncovered until tender, stirring occasionally. Drain. Place spaghetti onto warm serving dish; toss with prepared herb mixture. Place chicken around edge of platter; garnish with parsley sprigs. 4 to 6 servings.

Chicken Cacciatore

¼ cup olive oil
1 teaspoon salt
⅛ teaspoon pepper
3 pounds broiler-fryer chicken pieces
1 clove garlic, minced
2 medium onions, chopped
12 medium mushrooms, sliced
1 small green pepper, cut in large cubes
½ cup sliced black olives
1 8-ounce can tomato sauce
½ cup dry white or red wine
1 cup hot chicken broth
1 teaspoon basil
½ teaspoon dried mint
½ teaspoon oregano
1 small bay leaf
Cooked noodles
Freshly grated Romano cheese

Heat oil in 3-quart casserole. Salt and pepper chicken. Brown on both sides. Remove chicken; sauté garlic and onions until golden brown. Add mushrooms, green pepper and olives; place chicken on top of vegetables. Pour mixture of tomato sauce, wine, broth and herbs or 2½ cups Italian sauce over chicken. Bake in 350° oven 1 hour or until tender. Prepare noodles according to package directions. Drain. Toss with cheese and serve with chicken. 4 servings.

Goulash Soup

2 tablespoons butter
1½ cups finely chopped onion
2 cups cubed red and green sweet peppers
2 teaspoons finely chopped garlic
1 tablespoon caraway seeds
2 tablespoons paprika
2 tablespoons soy sauce
2 tablespoons whole wheat flour
1½ cups cubed potatoes
1 cup thinly sliced cabbage
1 1-pound can tomatoes
4 cups water
1 pound beef bones
2½ cups leftover beef, cut into ¾-inch pieces

Melt butter in a large saucepan. Add onions and peppers. Sauté until tender but not soft. Add caraway and minced garlic to onions and pepper. Sprinkle with paprika. Stir in soy sauce and flour. Simmer for 5 minutes, stirring constantly. Add potatoes, cabbage, tomatoes, water, meat and bones. Simmer 45 minutes. Remove bones and serve. Serves 8 to 10.

Here are some innovative and tasty solutions for less tender cuts of meat. We've also listed the various cuts of meat available and their general price range to help you know how best to stretch your meat dollar. As you savor the taste of Chicken with Curry Glaze or Boeuf a la Mode, savor the fact that you have also trimmed your food budget.

You don't need the most expensive cuts of meat to create a gourmet delight. If the high cost of meat is turning you away from making splendid fare, give some thought to the tips below and expand your food repertory by simply incorporating these ideas.

- Keep in mind that a freezer may be your best investment in order to take advantage of sales in all varieties of meat.

- Always use less expensive cuts of meat in soups, stews, and casseroles. A long, slow cooking time will tenderize the meat. We've included many delicious recipes for main dishes that utilize less expensive cuts of meat as a base and yet will taste like gourmet entrées!

- Know your herbs and spices . . . these additions can be the aromatic difference that can turn a super bargain into a super value.

- Marinades are especially helpful in tenderizing less expensive cuts of meat. Marinated meat should always be refrigerated prior to cooking unless the recipe specifies otherwise. Use a glass, porcelain or stainless steel dish as other materials may react with the acid content in the marinade.

- Poultry is still a good buy. Make it a better buy and segment or bone your own chicken.

- Roasting all meats at a low temperature cuts down on shrinkage and retains juices. Whatever the price per pound, use proper procedures to insure that you get the most out of your meat dollar.

Cuts of Meat

We've provided a list of the various cuts of meat available today and the price range into which they may fall. With this information, you will feel confident when approaching the meat counter that you will be getting good value for your meat dollar.

The United States Department of Agriculture has classified all cuts of meat into seven basic groups:

1. **Shoulder or Blade Cuts:** From the upper section of the shoulder, include part of the shoulder blade and muscle. Fairly inexpensive.

2. **Shoulder Arm Cuts:** From the lower part of the shoulder. Generally round in shape, these cuts include a round bone and part of a muscle. May include part of the ribs. Inexpensive.

3. **Breast Cuts:** From the chest portion of the animal. Consists of several thin muscles and layers of fat. Briskets and short rib cuts from this area. Can range from inexpensive to expensive.

4. **Rib Cuts:** From the rib area long the back, including portions of the ribs and backbone. The main feature here is tenderness and ease in carving. Expensive.

5. **Loin or Short Loin Cuts:** From the back between the ribs and hip, including the T-bone and two major muscles; the loin eye and the tenderloin. Tender and juicy. Expensive.

6. **Sirloin Cuts:** From the hip, sometimes including part of the backbone. Very tender and expensive.

7. **Leg, Round or Ham Cuts:** From the back leg, sometimes including a round bone. Can be moderate to expensive.

Remember, there are many different grades of meat, depending on how the animal has been raised. The higher the quality of meat, the more tender and flavorful it will be.

Beef Loaf

2 pounds ground beef
1 cup tomato sauce
1 egg
1 tablespoon Worcestershire sauce
1/3 cup chopped green pepper
2 medium onions, chopped
3/4 cup cracker crumbs, finely crushed
1 teaspoon salt
1/4 teaspoon pepper
1/4 cup catsup

Combine ground beef, tomato sauce, egg, Worcestershire sauce, green pepper, onions, cracker crumbs, salt and pepper. Mix lightly but thoroughly. Shape meat mixture into a 9 x 4 x 3-inch loaf and place on a rack in an open roasting pan. Bake in a 350° oven for 1 hour and 15 minutes. Pour catsup over top of beef loaf and continue baking 10 to 15 minutes or until done. Makes 6 to 8 servings.

Chicken with Curry Glaze

2 3-pound chickens, cut up
6 tablespoons flour
1½ teaspoons salt
1 teaspoon ginger
3/4 cup butter
Curry Glaze (optional)

Shake pieces of chicken in a bag with the flour, salt and ginger. Melt the butter in a baking pan and roll chicken in butter, coating well. Arrange skin side up in a single layer and bake uncovered for 20 minutes at 400°. Turn chicken, brush with more butter and bake another 20 minutes. Brush chicken with glaze and bake an additional 20 minutes untill golden. Serve with rice. Serves 6 to 8.

Curry Glaze

6 slices bacon
1 medium apple, peeled and diced
2 tablespoons flour
1 tablespoon curry powder
1 tablespoon sugar
1 cup condensed beef broth
2 tablespoons catsup
2 tablespoons lemon juice

Dice bacon and fry gently until brown. Drain bacon. Add remaining ingredients and cook over medium heat, stirring constantly until thickened.

Boeuf à la Mode

2 pounds chuck roast, cubed
2 medium onions, quartered
2 stalks celery, quartered
4 potatoes, pared and quartered
2 carrots, peeled and quartered
1/4 cup dry bread crumbs
1 teaspoon salt
1/2 teaspoon pepper
1 teaspoon thyme
1 1-pound can tomatoes and juice
1 teaspoon Worcestershire sauce
3/4 cup dry red wine
1 10-ounce package frozen peas
1 4-ounce can mushrooms

In a large casserole with a cover, combine all ingredients except peas and mushrooms. Place in a 325° oven for 3 hours. Add peas and mushrooms and bake, uncovered, for an additional 30 minutes. Serves 4 to 6.

Sweet-Sour Pork

1½ pounds lean pork, cut into bite-size pieces
3 tablespoons vegetable oil
1 medium onion, chopped
1 green pepper, chopped
1 rib celery, sliced
1 clove garlic, minced
Salt, pepper

Sauté onion, pepper and celery in oil for a few minutes. Remove from pan and set aside to use in sauce. In the same pan, brown pork, seasoning with garlic, salt and pepper to taste. Prepare sauce and pour over pork; cover and simmer for 45 minutes, or until tender and well done. Serve with rice. Serves 4 to 6.

Sauce

3/4 cup sugar
1/4 cup vinegar
1 tablespoon soy sauce
1 tablespoon lemon juice
1 tablespoon catsup
1 tablespoon cornstarch
1/4 cup chicken broth

Combine sugar, vinegar, soy sauce, lemon juice and catsup. Mix well. Dissolve cornstarch in chicken broth, stirring until mixture thickens and clears. Add onion, pepper, celery, and catsup mixture.

Pork with Sauerkraut

1 tablespoon butter
2 tablespoons brown sugar
4 tablespoons chopped onion
½ cup leftover pork gravy
1 8-ounce can sauerkraut
1 teaspoon caraway seed
¼ teaspoon salt
8 slices leftover roast pork

Combine butter with sugar in a large sauce-pan. Cook slowly over low heat; stir constantly until sugar is melted. Add onion and simmer covered for 5 minutes. Add gravy, sauerkraut, salt and caraway seed; bring to a boil, and stir. Add pork to sauerkraut, and simmer covered for 10 minutes. Serves 8.

Scalloped Pork Chops

6 to 8 pork chops
1 tablespoon mustard
1 tablespoon salad oil
4 to 6 medium potatoes, peeled and sliced thin
1 small onion, chopped
1 can cream of celery soup
1 soup can milk
1 to 2 teaspoons salt
¼ teaspoon pepper
½ teaspoon marjoram

Spread a little mustard on each chop and brown chops in oil. In a 2 to 3-quart casserole, arrange potatoes, onion and chops in layers. Mix soup, milk, salt, pepper and marjoram together and pour over potatoes and chops. Cover and bake in a preheated 350° oven for 1½ to 2 hours. Make 4 to 6 servings.

Sukiyaki

3 tablespoons vegetable oil
1 medium sliced onion
4 large sliced mushrooms
½ pound thinly sliced beef, uncooked
¼ pound fresh spinach
3 5-inch pieces celery, thinly sliced
4 tablespoons soy sauce
2 tablespoons sugar
½ can consommé
4 scallions

Sauté onion in oil; add mushrooms and meat, cook 2 minutes. Add spinach and cook 1 minute. Add celery and cook 1 minute. Cut scallions lengthwise into thin pieces. Add to mixture. Add soy sauce, cook 1 minute. Add sugar and consommé and cook 2 minutes. Makes 2 to 3 servings. Repeat as often as necessary.

Barbecued Short Ribs

4 pounds beef short ribs
2 teaspoons salt
¼ teaspoon pepper
1 8-ounce can tomato sauce
¼ cup catsup
⅓ cup brown sugar
¼ cup vinegar
2 tablespoons prepared mustard
½ cup chopped onion
1 clove garlic, minced
1 tablespoon chili powder

Place short ribs in covered frying pan on grill and cook slowly for 1½ hours, turning occasionally. Season with salt and pepper. Combine tomato sauce, catsup, brown sugar, vinegar, mustard, onion, garlic and chili powder in saucepan and simmer 5 minutes. Remove each short rib from pan, dip in sauce to coat all sides and place on grill, brushing with sauce and turning occasionally for 20 to 30 minutes or until done. 4 servings.

Spiced Kettle of Beef and Vegetables

2 pounds boneless beef chuck, cut in 1-inch cubes
½ cup flour
1 tablespoon salt
½ teaspoon pepper
½ teaspoon paprika
2 tablespoons shortening or vegetable oil
1 cup chopped onion
6 cups water
Garni (1 clove and 1 teaspoon pickling spice in cloth)
3 cups drained, canned tomatoes
2 cups diced carrots
1 cup sliced celery
3 cups diced potatoes
1 cup green peas
1 teaspoon sugar
2 teaspoons salt
¼ teaspoon pepper
3 tablespoons cornstarch blended with ¼ cup cold water

Dredge beef cubes in mixture of flour, salt, pepper and paprika. Brown in fat on all sides in large heavy kettle. Add onion and brown lightly. Add water and garni. Simmer, covered for 30 minutes. Add vegetables and seasonings. Simmer, uncovered, for 30 minutes or until done. Blend some of the hot gravy into the cornstarch mixture and stir into stew until thick. Serves 8 to 10.

Variations on a Theme

We take the ordinary burger, frankfurter and sandwich and do extraordinary things with them. These are just a few suggestions . . . use your imagination to find more variations on a theme!

Better Burgers

With the cost of beef at a high level in most areas of the country and the need for quick and tasty meals increasing, hamburger is a welcome guest at mealtime. We've included easy additions to help you give new zest to that old standby, the all-American burger.

In the burger patty . . .
- minced onion
- minced green pepper
- a dash of Worcestershire per burger
- a sprinkling of oregano, chives or dill
- a dash of chili or curry powder
- a dash of soy sauce

Regal toppings
- onion rounds
- sliced cherry tomatoes
- sliced avocado
- slices of bacon
- spoonful of baked beans
- homemade dills, sliced or relish
- green pepper rounds
- mushrooms, fresh or sautéed
- alfalfa sprouts
- green or black olives, sliced
- grated carrot, red cabbage and/or radishes

Sauces
- chili sauce
- horseradish
- barbecue
- sour cream
- chutney
- extra dip such as French onion or guacamole

The cheeses . . .
- American or Cheddar cheese
- Swiss
- mozzarella
- Monterey jack
- havarti with caraway
- blue or Gorgonzola

The rolls . . . vary the server
- hard rolls
- onion rolls
- potato buns
- rye bread
- brown bread

Fantastic Franks

Frankfurters are a favorite of kids all ages. Here are some new serving suggestions for your menus.

1. Parboil frankfurters; then place on broiler pan. Split and fill with a mixture of minced onion, diced green pepper, crumbled bacon, and grated Cheddar cheese. Broil till bubbly.

2. Dice frankfurters in omelets for a tasty addition and complete one-dish meal.

3. After grilling or broiling, split frankfurters and fill each with a tablespoon of heated sauerkraut. Top with Swiss cheese. Broil till cheese melts.

4. Vary the sauces you serve: try chili sauce, guacamole, horseradish or barbecue sauce.

5. Use sliced franks in scalloped potatoes instead of ham.

6. Add diced frankfurters to green beans or corn to entice kids to eat their vegetables.

7. Place a spoonful of baked beans and a slice of crisp bacon on top of each frankfurter in its bun.

8. Place cooked and sliced frankfurters on toasted English muffins. Top with slices of tomato and Cheddar cheese. Broil until cheese melts.

9. Garnish German Potato Salad with slices of frankfurters.

10. Use a package of refrigerated biscuits. Roll each portion of dough into a rectangle. Place frankfurter in center of dough and secure edges firmly. Bake at 350° for 15 to 20 minutes until golden.

11. Add sliced frankfurters to macaroni and cheese. Heat thoroughly.

12. For a super one-dish dinner, cook sauerkraut and small red potatoes in a covered skillet until potatoes are done. Prior to serving, add one dill pickle and frankfurter for each person and heat thoroughly. Serve with buttered rye bread.

Savory Sandwiches

Beef Steak Sandwiches Mediterranean

    1 8-ounce can tomato sauce
    ½ cup grated Parmesan cheese
    2 teaspoons instant minced onion
    1 teaspoon oregano
      Dash garlic powder
    2 large English muffins
    4 beef cubed steaks
    2 tablespoons lard or drippings
    4 slices mozzarella cheese
    ½ teaspoon oregano
    ½ teaspoon basil
    4 large stuffed green olives, sliced

Combine tomato sauce, Parmesan cheese, onion, oregano and garlic powder. Simmer 5 minutes. Split and toast English muffins. Brown cubed steaks on both sides in lard over moderate heat. Place each browned steak on English muffin half. Spread 2 tablespoons tomato mixture on each steak. Cover each with a slice of mozzarella cheese. Mix oregano and basil and sprinkle a little on each slice. Arrange slices of stuffed green olives on tops. Broil 3 inches from heat for about 5 minutes or until cheese melts. Serves 4.

Tuna "Franks"

    1 7-ounce can tuna
    3 hard-boiled eggs, diced
    1 cup diced Cheddar cheese
    ½ cup mayonnaise
    2 teaspoons chopped sweet pickle
    2 teaspoons chopped green pepper
    1 teaspoon minced onion
    2 tablespoons chopped stuffed olives
    ¾ teaspoon salt
    ½ teaspoon pepper
    10 frankfurter rolls

Combine all ingredients except rolls. Split rolls and fill with tuna mixture; wrap each in foil. Bake in a 375° oven for 20 minutes. Serve in foil. Serves 10.

Cornish Pasties

      Pastry for double-crust pie (page 17)
    2 medium potatoes, peeled and cubed
    1 small onion, minced
    ½ pound lean, thick pork steak, cubed
    2 medium carrots, peeled and diced
    ½ pound lean, thick round steak, cubed
      Salt, pepper
      Butter

Divide pastry in half. Roll each half into a circle. Combine remaining ingredients, ex-

cept butter. Place one half of ingredients on one half of each pastry circle. Dot with butter and fold other half of pastry over ingredients. Pinch edges together firmly. Pierce top several times with fork. Bake at 450° for 45 minutes until golden.

Barbecue Beef

    ½ pound ground beef
    2 tablespoons chopped onion
    2 tablespoons chopped green pepper
    1 stalk celery, cut fine
    ½ cup catsup
    ½ cup water
    1 tablespoon vinegar
    1½ teaspoons Worcestershire sauce
    ½ teaspoon prepared mustard
    1 tablespoon brown sugar
    ½ teaspoon salt
    ⅛ teaspoon allspice

Brown beef until crumbly but not dry. Before beef is done, push to one side of pan and sauté onion, green pepper and celery. Combine remaining ingredients and pour over meat. Cover pan tightly and simmer for 30 minutes. Serve hot over toasted buns. Serves 6 to 8.

Favorite Hero

    ½ loaf Vienna bread
    ¼ cup (½ stick) butter, softened
    2 tablespoons prepared mustard
    1 22-ounce jar baked beans
    1 cup (4 ounces) shredded Cheddar cheese
    1 small onion, finely chopped
    2 tablespoons light brown sugar
    6 frankfurters, split lengthwise
    3 1-ounce slices Cheddar cheese
      Cucumber pickle slices

Cut bread in half lengthwise. With fingers scoop out bread crumbs leaving shell ¾-inch thick. Place bread on baking sheet. Combine butter and mustard; spread on cut surfaces of bread. In bowl combine beans, cheese, onion and sugar; spoon on bread, filling hollow and covering to edges. Place frankfurters diagonally on beans. Bake in preheated 350° oven, 25 minutes or until beans are bubbly and bread is warm. Cut cheese slices in half. Top each frankfurter with a slice of cheese. Place pickle slices on each cheese slice. Return to oven; bake until cheese starts to melt. Serves 6.

Saving Time

- Quick and Easy Meals for Two
- Family Dinners in 30 Minutes
- Company Entrees in 60 Minutes or Less!
- Last Minute Additions for Memorable Meals
- Microwave It!

Although you have a busy schedule, with many job and home responsibilities, you can learn to set priorities and organize your time to make family meals and company entertaining easier. Here are some time-saving tips to use in conjunction with the quick recipes in this chapter:

1. Try to learn about and use conveniences and special services that don't cost extra money. For example, catalog and at-home shopping are ways to streamline your schedule and save time.

2. Plan your menus each week and shop *only once*. As you list special foods needed for the week, also check your staple foods and replenish as necessary.

3. Write your shopping list according to the floor plan of your favorite supermarket, listing foods in the order in which they are arranged in the store. You will make a much faster trip through the store instead of wandering back and forth between the aisles.

4. Use freezer and storage spaces well. If you take advantage of sales and coupons to stock up and save money, you can avoid many of those "emergency" trips to the supermarket when unexpected company arrives. Note your favorite recipes in "Company Entrees" (page 54) and have those ingredients on hand.

5. Organize your kitchen to save steps. Keep your most-needed cookbooks and utensils in the specific place where you use them. You will find that you develop an efficient pattern in the working process.

6. Plan ahead and have a "cooking marathon" once or twice a month. Prepare a few entrees, breads, cakes or cookies and then freeze them, plainly labeled, in measured servings. Freeze some whole-family portions and some individual servings. Try to double the recipe when you cook a favorite soup, stew or spaghetti sauce; you can freeze one-half for later use.

7. "Convenience foods" are worth their extra cost when time is short, and many taste as good as homemade. A stock of frozen pastry shells can make a quiche or a dessert pie quick and easy.

8. Save salad preparation time: wash and tear salad greens for two meals at once. Dry greens carefully and store one-half without dressing in an air-tight container for the next meal.

9. As a homemaker, with or without a job, your greatest difficulty may be finding leisure time. Try to set aside one afternoon or evening a week in which all your responsibilities are forgotten. (Make plans for the kids to visit with friends or find a babysitter.) It is important to have relaxation time for yourself, so that you can keep pace with a challenging schedule.

Here are some delicious recipes for the two of you that are quick and easy to prepare. If you are cooking for one, most can be prepared, enjoyed for one meal, and then frozen for another.

Appetizers

Peppercorn Dip

2 tablespoons green peppercorns
or 1 teaspoon black pepper,
1 teaspoon vinegar and ¼ teaspoon salt
1 large clove garlic, crushed
⅓ cup Dijon mustard
1 egg
1 cup olive oil
Chopped parsley

Blend peppercorns, garlic and mustard in a blender until smooth. Add egg; blend until smooth. Gradually add oil by pouring in a thin stream and blending until smooth. Garnish with chopped parsley. 1½ cups.

Curry Canapés

¾ cup Cheddar cheese, shredded
½ cup ripe olives, chopped
¼ cup chopped scallions
¼ cup mayonnaise
½ teaspoon curry powder
1 small loaf party rye

In a small bowl mix all ingredients together. Spread on party rye cut cornerwise. Broil until bubbly. Spread will stay fresh for one month when refrigerated.

Pizza Fondue

1 onion, chopped
½ pound ground beef
2 10½-ounce cans pizza sauce (or tomato sauce)
1 tablespoon cornstarch
1½ teaspoons fennel seed
1½ teaspoons oregano
¼ teaspoon garlic powder
10 ounces grated Cheddar cheese
1 cup grated mozzarella cheese

Brown onion and ground beef in a large sauce pan. Mix pizza sauce and cornstarch together and add to meat. Add fennel seed, oregano and garlic powder to this mixture. Simmer 30 minutes. Just before serving, add Cheddar and mozzarella cheese. Stir over medium heat until cheeses are melted. Pour into fondue pot. Serve with garlic bread cubes or French bread cubes. May be reheated on English muffins as a sandwich.

Soups

Potato Soup

2 medium-sized potatoes, pared and diced
2 slices onion
1 teaspoon salt
1 cup hot milk
Dash pepper
1 stalk celery, sliced very fine
⅓ cup boiling water

Combine potatoes, onion and salt in a saucepan; add boiling water. Cover and cook until potatoes are tender. Do not drain. Mash potatoes with a fork; add milk, pepper, and celery. More milk may be added if soup is too thick. Serve hot.

Tomato Soup

1 tablespoon butter
2 onions, sliced
2 large tomatoes, peeled
1 cup chicken broth
¾ tablespoon lemon juice
1 teaspoon sugar
½ teaspoon salt
Dash pepper

Add onions and tomatoes to melted butter and simmer until tender. Add remaining ingredients; bring to a boil and simmer until ready to serve.

Clam Chowder

1 slice bacon
2 tablespoons diced onion
¼ teaspoon salt
Dash pepper
1 8-ounce can minced clams
1 cup milk
1 tablespoon butter
½ cup water
1 small potato, pared and diced

Sauté bacon until crisp in a small saucepan. Add onion and cook until tender. Add potatoes to water, and season with salt and pepper. Cook until potatoes are tender. Add clams with liquid, milk and butter. Cook for 3 minutes. Simmer, until ready to serve.

Cheese Mushroom Soup

2 tablespoons butter
2 teaspoons fresh lemon juice
¼ pound fresh mushrooms, sliced
1 small onion, chopped
1 tablespoon all-purpose flour
2 teaspoons chicken stock base
¼ teaspoon dill weed
2 cups milk
1 egg, slightly beaten
¾ cup Cheddar cheese, shredded

Melt butter in a 1-quart saucepan; add lemon juice, mushrooms and onion. Sauté until onions are tender. Stir in flour, chicken stock base and dill. Cook over low heat until mixture is smooth. Remove from heat. Stir in milk. Heat to boiling, stirring constantly. Boil 1 minute stirring constantly. Blend a small amount of hot mixture into egg; return all to pan. Cook 1 minute. Remove from heat; stir in cheese until melted. If necessary, return to low heat to finish melting cheese. Do not boil. Makes 3 cups.

Salads

Spinach Salad Deluxe

1 pound fresh spinach, washed, dried and shredded
4 to 6 green onions, chopped
4 slices bacon, fried and crumbled
½ cup mayonnaise
½ cup sour cream
3 tablespoons grated Parmesan cheese
Bacon to garnish

Toss spinach, onions and bacon. Mix mayonnaise, sour cream and cheese together. Toss with salad. Garnish with bacon and serve. Serves 2 to 4.

Waldorf Salad

1 small pear, diced
1 small eating apple, diced
1 stalk celery, diced
2 tablespoons chopped pecans
¼ cup salad dressing
1 tablespoon orange juice
2 lettuce leaves

Mix together pear, apple, celery and nuts. Blend salad dressing and orange juice. Add to salad mixture; toss to mix. Serve on lettuce.

Entrees

Chicken Livers

½ to ¾ pound chicken livers
¼ cup all-purpose flour
1 teaspoon salt
⅛ teaspoon pepper
1 teaspoon oregano, crushed
2 tablespoons vegetable oil
Lemon juice

Dredge livers in flour mixed with salt, pepper and oregano. Heat oil in skillet. Add livers; fry 10 minutes, turning frequently. Squeeze fresh lemon juice over top before serving.

Apple Pancake

1 apple
4 tablespoons butter
2 tablespoons sugar
¼ teaspoon cinnamon
¼ teaspoon nutmeg (optional)
1 cup Bisquick
⅔ cup milk
1 egg
1 tablespoon sugar

Core apple; do not peel. Cut into twelve slices. Melt butter in 9-inch iron skillet. Stir in cinnamon, 2 tablespoons sugar and apple slices; sauté until tender. Combine Bisquick, milk, egg and remaining sugar until just moistened. Pour over apple slices. Turn heat to low and cook 10 minutes until surface of pancake looks dull. Place under broiler for a couple of minutes until lightly browned. To serve, turn upside down on plate and pass extra butter and syrup. Serves 2 to 4.

Shrimply Delightful

1½ pounds raw deveined shrimp
2 tablespoons lemon juice
½ cup melted butter
½ cup bread crumbs
½ teaspoon minced garlic or onion
2 tablespoons chopped parsley
1 tablespoon Parmesan cheese
1 tablespoon oregano

Arrange shrimp on 9" buttered pie plate; sprinkle with lemon juice. Combine melted butter with bread crumbs, garlic or onion, and parsley. Spoon over shrimp. Bake uncovered, at 350° for 15 minutes. Add cheese. Broil 3 minutes to brown the crumbs. Garnish with parsley and lemon.

Cornish Game Hens

        2 (1-pound size) Cornish Game Hens
    ½ teaspoon salt
    ¼ teaspoon pepper
    6 tablespoons butter
    1 teaspoon lemon juice
    ⅛ teaspoon paprika

Sprinkle salt and pepper in each hen. Tie legs together with string. Combine 4 table-spoons butter with lemon juice and paprika, stirring well to make basting sauce. Brown hens in remaining butter in medium skillet. Put hens in large roasting pan, without rack; brush with basting sauce. Roast in a pre-heated 450° oven 40 minutes or until tender.

Lasagne

    3 ounces lasagne noodles
      Dash oregano
    1 8-ounce can spaghetti sauce with meat
    ½ cup cottage cheese
    3 ounces sliced mozzarella cheese
      Dash salt, pepper

Cook lasagne noodles as package directs. Add oregano, salt, and pepper to spaghetti sauce. Alternate layers of noodles, cottage cheese, mozzarella, and sauce. Bake in a preheated 375° oven 30 minutes.

Stir-Fried Shrimp and Pea Pods

    3 tablespoons safflower or corn oil
    ½ teaspoon ground ginger or ½ teaspoon
      finely chopped fresh gingerroot
    1 clove garlic, minced
    ¾ pound uncooked, cleaned shrimp
    1 6-ounce package frozen or ½ pound fresh
      pea pods
    ¼ to ½ cup sliced bamboo shoots (optional)
    ¼ cup instant chicken bouillon
    1 tablespoon soy sauce
    1 teaspoon sugar
    1 tablespoon dry sherry (optional)

Heat oil in wok or frying pan with ginger and garlic. Add shrimp and stir fry 1½ min-utes. Add pea pods and bamboo shoots; stir fry 2 minutes. Add chicken bouillon, soy sauce, sugar and sherry and stir fry 2 min-utes. Serve on hot cooked rice.

Broiled Steak with Mushroom Topping

    1-inch thick beef steak (your favorite cut)
      Salt, pepper

Broiling Time: (Each Side)

    5 to 7 min . . . . . .rare
    8 to 9 min . . . . . .medium
    10 to 12 min . . . . . .well done

Season one side with salt and pepper. Broil. Turn. Season second side. When broiling is completed, serve with Mushroom Topping.

Mushroom Topping

    ½ pound mushrooms
    3 tablespoons butter

Wash mushrooms; drain. Cut lengthwise in thin slices. Melt butter; add mushrooms. Cover; cook over low heat 3 to 4 minutes. Uncover; continue cooking about 5 minutes.

Veal Piccata

    4 veal scallops, pounded thin
      Flour
      Salt and pepper
    6 tablespoons butter
    2 tablespoons olive oil
    3 tablespoons lemon juice
    2 tablespoons snipped parsley
    1 8-ounce package green noodles

Cook noodles according to package direc-tions while preparing veal. Lightly dust veal with flour seasoned with salt and pepper. Heat 4 tablespoons butter and oil in a large skillet over medium heat until bubbly. Quickly brown veal on both sides. Remove veal from pan to warm platter. Add lemon juice, parsley and remaining butter to skillet, stirring until just heated. Arrange veal on noodles and pour sauce over all. Garnish with lemon slices. Serves 2 to 4.

Agneau Grille

    8 lamb chops, slash fat
    ½ teaspoon garlic powder
    1 tablespoon rosemary
    1 teaspoon salt
    ½ teaspoon pepper

Crush together garlic powder, rosemary, salt and pepper. Press a little into each chop. Let stand 30 minutes. Broil 5 minutes on each side. Makes 4 servings.

Veal Steaks with Tomato Sauce

1 tablespoon butter
¼ cup chopped onion
2 veal steaks
4 ounces tomato juice
¼ cup water
⅛ teaspoon salt
Dash pepper
⅛ teaspoon oregano

Sauté onions in melted butter; remove from pan. Add meat and brown on both sides. Add onions, tomato juice, water, oregano, salt and pepper; simmer until tender, about 1 hour.

Hamburger Stroganoff

½ pound ground beef
2 tablespoons butter
2 tablespoons sliced mushrooms
¼ cup chopped onion
¼ clove garlic, minced
½ teaspoon salt
⅛ teaspoon pepper
¼ teaspoon Worcestershire sauce
1 tablespoon flour
2½ tablespoons chili sauce
6 tablespoons sour cream
Spaghetti

Brown ground beef in half of the butter. Add remaining butter, mushrooms, onion, garlic, salt and pepper; sauté until onions are golden and tender. Add Worcestershire sauce. Stir in flour, then chili sauce. Just before serving, blend in sour cream. Serve hot over cooked spaghetti.

Clams and Shells

1 large clove garlic, halved
⅛ cup vegetable oil
2 tablespoons lemon juice
2 tablespoons butter or margarine
2 cans clams (crushed or whole) and juice
½ teaspoon salt
½ teaspoon basil, crushed
¼ teaspoon pepper
2 teaspoons minced parsley, fresh or dried
1 7-ounce package seashell pasta, cooked
¼ cup melted unsalted butter
1 cup grated Parmesan cheese

Brown garlic in oil; discard garlic. Stir in next 7 ingredients. Simmer 10 minutes, stirring occasionally. Cook and drain pasta; toss with butter. Mix with sauce and garnish with Parmesan cheese. Serves 2 to 4.

Vegetables

Potatoes au Gratin

2 tablespoons butter
2½ tablespoons onion, chopped
¼ cup milk
6 ounces condensed Cheddar cheese soup
2 tablespoons fine, dry, bread crumbs
2 cups cooked, cubed potatoes
2½ tablespoons chopped pimiento

Sauté onion in 1 tablespoon melted butter until tender. Mix in cheese soup and milk. Melt remaining butter and mix with bread crumbs. In a casserole dish, arrange potatoes, soup mixture and pimiento in layers. Top with bread crumbs. Bake in a preheated 375° oven for 30 minutes.

Wild Rice

1 cup wild rice
1 teaspoon salt
¾ cup cooked mushrooms, chopped

Wash rice and drain. Combine rice and salt with 6 cups cold water in a large saucepan. Cover and bring to a boil. Uncover and boil for 50 minutes or until rice is tender. Drain rice and return to saucepan. Add mushrooms and simmer 10 to 15 minutes.

Broccoli or Asparagus
with Instant Hollandaise Sauce

1 pound fresh broccoli or asparagus or
1 10-ounce package frozen broccoli or asparagus
1 teaspoon chicken bouillon crystals
Water

Place broccoli or asparagus in a steamer with a small amount of water (about ¼ cup). Sprinkle with chicken bouillon crystals. Steam until tender-crisp, 10 to 15 minutes. (Time will vary according to the density of vegetables.) Serve with Hollandaise Sauce.

Instant Hollandaise Sauce

1 cup sour cream
1 cup mayonnaise
¼ cup lemon juice

Combine all ingredients and blend together. Heat slowly and serve hot over asparagus or broccoli.

Broccoli Casserole with Noodles

4 ounces noodles
1½ tablespoons butter
¼ teaspoon salt
Dash pepper
1 bunch broccoli, cleaned and cooked
½ cup sliced mushrooms
1 cup cooked chicken, sliced
1 cup sour cream

Cook noodles as package directs. In melted butter, mix salt and pepper with noodles. In a separate dish mix cooked broccoli with mushrooms. Combine chicken with sour cream. In a small casserole dish, arrange half of noodles; add meat mixture, and broccoli. Top with rest of noodles. Bake in a 350° oven for 30 minutes.

Quick Breads

Lemon Nut Bread

2½ cups flour
1 cup sugar
3½ teaspoons baking powder
½ teaspoon baking soda
½ teaspoon salt
½ cup water
⅓ cup melted shortening
2 eggs, beaten
1½ tablespoons freshly grated lemon peel
½ cup freshly squeezed lemon juice
½ cup chopped nuts
½ cup raisins

In a large bowl, sift together dry ingredients. Combine water, shortening, eggs, lemon peel and juice; add to flour mixture. Stir just until blended. Stir in nuts and raisins. Pour into a greased 9 x 5 x 3-inch loaf pan. Bake in a 350° oven for 1 hour and 15 minutes or until toothpick inserted in center comes out clean. Cool 10 minutes; remove from pan. Cool in wire rack. Refrigerate and use as desired. Makes 1 loaf.

Crusty French Onion Bread

1 loaf French bread
¼ pound softened butter or margarine
2 to 4 tablespoons dry onion soup mix
¼ cup snipped parsley

Diagonally cut bread into thick slices. Combine remaining ingredients and spread on sliced bread. Reassemble bread, wrap in foil and bake in a preheated 400° oven for 15 minutes.

Mellow Muffins

1 cup seedless raisins
2 cups sifted flour
⅓ cup brown sugar, firmly packed
3 teaspoons baking powder
1 teaspoon cinnamon
½ teaspoon salt
¼ teaspoon baking soda
1 egg
⅔ cup milk
½ cup (1 medium) mashed ripe banana
¼ cup melted margarine or butter

Combine first 7 ingredients; set aside. Combine egg, milk, banana and margarine; mix well and add to dry ingredients. Stir until all flour is moistened. Fill greased muffin pans two-thirds full. Bake in a 400° oven 20 to 25 minutes. Serve immediately or freeze and use as desired. Makes 12 medium muffins.

Desserts

Peach Delight

2 peaches
1 teaspoon lemon juice
3 tablespoons sugar
½ cup whipping cream
2 teaspoons sugar
½ teaspoon vanilla
2 small sponge cakes, about 4 inches in diameter, cut in small pieces

Peel and slice peaches. Add lemon juice and 3 tablespoons sugar. Let stand while preparing other ingredients. Whip cream; add 2 teaspoons sugar and vanilla. Fold together cake pieces, whipped cream and peaches.

Individual Apple Crisp

⅔ cup pared and sliced baking apples
2 teaspoons water
⅛ cup granulated sugar
⅛ cup brown sugar
Dash salt
⅛ teaspoon nutmeg
⅛ teaspoon cinnamon
½ of ⅓ cup flour
⅛ cup butter

Place half of the apples and 1 teaspoon water in each of two custard cups. Combine sugars, salt, spices and flour in a bowl; cut in butter with pastry blender. Sprinkle crumb mixture in each custard cup. Place cups on cookie sheet and bake in a preheated 375° oven about 25 minutes. Serve warm or cold. Garnish with whipped cream.

This is a very special assortment of recipes to save you time in meal preparation. All recipes are geared for a family of four or more. Some, such as Lobster Thermidor, are so delicious that you might even want to have company over to savor every bite with you! Others, such as Swedish Meatballs, may be adapted to bite-sized appetizers, ready in a matter of minutes! Try every one . . . this is a family-pleasing selection of quick and easy dinners!

Swedish Meatballs

2 pounds ground beef
1½ cups fine bread crumbs
1 teaspoon salt
Pepper
¼ cup milk
¼ cup applesauce
2 eggs
1 teaspoon minced onion
¼ teaspoon nutmeg
3 tablespoons butter

Combine ingredients except butter, mix well and form into 48 small balls. Brown in butter, then add water to simmer (about 2 cups). Cook, covered, for 15 minutes. Serve over rice or noodles. These freeze well and can be made smaller to use as hors d'oeuvres.

Lobster Thermidor

¼ cup butter, melted
½ cup flour
1 teaspoon salt
Pinch of cayenne pepper
¼ teaspoon dry mustard
2½ cups milk
½ pound fresh mushrooms, sliced
¼ cup butter
4 cups cooked lobster (bite-sized pieces)
2 tablespoons dry sherry
⅓ cup grated Parmesan cheese

To the melted butter, add flour, salt, cayenne and mustard, stirring constantly until smooth. Add the milk slowly, stirring constantly. Cook until thickened. Remove from heat. Sauté the mushrooms in the ¼ cup butter. Add mushrooms, lobster and sherry to the sauce. Mix well and pour into a buttered casserole. Sprinkle the top with Parmesan cheese. Bake in a preheated 400° oven about 15 minutes until bubbly. Makes 6 to 8 servings, but recipe may be cut in half.

Variation: Add ¼ to ½ cup grated Swiss cheese to cream sauce.

Tuna Oriental

1 13¼-ounce can pineapple chunks
2 2-ounce envelopes sweet and sour sauce mix
1 medium green pepper
2 ribs celery, sliced (optional)
2 6½-ounce cans tuna
1 can bamboo shoots
1 can sliced water chestnuts

Fifteen minutes before serving drain pineapple; set aside chunks. Add enough water to juice to make 2 cups liquid. In saucepan, heat sauce mix and juice until thickened, stirring occasionally. Add green pepper and celery and cook 5 minutes. Add tuna, pineapple chunks, bamboo shoots and water chestnuts; cook until thoroughly heated. Serve with rice. Makes 4 servings.

Sole Gratinée

8 to 10 small fillets of sole, sprinkled with salt, pepper and paprika
1¼ cup dry vermouth
3 tablespoons flour
3 tablespoons softened butter
½ cup light cream
2 to 3 tomatoes, sliced
½ cup grated Swiss cheese
2 tablespoons chopped parsley

Arrange fillets in 8 x 10-inch shallow baking dish; they will overlap. Pour 1 cup dry vermouth over and poach for 20 minutes in a 350° oven until fish flakes easily with a fork. When fish is done, pour poaching liquid into saucepan. Bring to a simmer. Combine flour and butter to make a paste and add to poaching liquid, stirring with a whisk until it thickens. Add remaining vermouth and cream; cook, stirring, until mixture coats spoon. Arrange sliced tomatoes on top of fish. Pour sauce over all. Sprinkle with cheese and parsley; broil 4 to 6 minutes until cheese melts and sauce bubbles. Serves 4.

Monterrey Bake

1 pound lean ground beef
1 teaspoon garlic powder
1 teaspoon onion powder
1½ teaspoons salt
¼ teaspoon liquid hot pepper
1 tablespoon lemon juice
½ cup mayonnaise
3 cups cooked rice
1 cup sliced celery
½ cup chopped green pepper
2 medium tomatoes, cut in eighths
1 cup crushed corn chips

Sauté meat with garlic and onion powders in a lightly greased skillet about 5 minutes, or until done. Blend salt, liquid pepper, lemon juice and mayonnaise. Add this mixture and remaining ingredients to ground beef. Turn into a greased 2-quart casserole. Top with corn chips. Bake at 375° for 25 minutes. Makes 6 servings.

Chicken Vermouth

4 whole chicken breasts
¼ cup butter
1 clove garlic, minced
1 teaspoon salt
¼ teaspoon pepper
½ pound mushrooms, sliced
1 tablespoon lemon juice
¾ cup dry vermouth
¼ cup snipped parsley

Sauté breasts in butter. Add garlic, salt, pepper and lemon juice. Heap mushrooms on top, pour on vermouth, cover and cook for 20 to 30 minutes or until chicken is fork tender. Add a little vermouth if more liquid is needed. Sprinkle with parsley just before serving. Serves 6.

Curried Ham Steak

2 ham steaks, ¼ to ½ inch thick
¼ cup butter
¼ cup brown sugar
1 tablespoon curry powder
¼ cup raisins
1 1-pound can pineapple slices, drained
1 1-pound can apricot halves, drained
1 1-pound can pear halves, drained

Melt together butter and brown sugar. Stir in curry powder. Place ham steaks in a large shallow baking dish. Top with fruit. Pour brown sugar sauce over all and bake for 30 minutes in a 350° oven until it sizzles. Serves 4 to 6.

Veal, Ham and Cheese

4 veal cutlets, ¼ inch thick
4 tablespoons butter or margarine
¼ cup dry sherry
4 thin slices of prosciutto or cooked ham
½ pound Port du Salut or Swiss cheese cut in 4 slices

Using a large skillet, lightly brown veal on both sides in butter over medium heat. Remove skillet from heat; add sherry and stir, scraping the bottom of the pan to release brown bits. Arrange veal on bottom of skillet; add a slice of ham and cheese to each cutlet. Cover and cook over low heat 5 to 10 minutes. Serves 4.

Pepper Steak

2 pounds round steak in ½" strips
3 tablespoons oil
1 medium onion, diced
¼ cup soy sauce
¼ cup sugar
1 teaspoon salt
Pepper
¼ teaspoon ginger
2 green peppers, cut in strips
4 tomatoes, quartered
¼ cup water
1 tablespoon cornstarch
1 cup bean sprouts (optional)

Brown strips of round steak in oil. Add onion, soy sauce, sugar, seasonings, green pepper, tomatoes, and water. Cook for 15 minutes. Mix cornstarch with a little water and add. Cook for 5 minutes. Bean sprouts may be added last if desired. Serves 4 to 6.

Veal Paprikash

2 pounds veal, cubed
¼ cup flour
½ teaspoon salt
¼ teaspoon pepper
4 tablespoons safflower or corn oil
2 teaspoons paprika
2 onions, sliced
1 cup instant chicken bouillon
½ to ¾ cup sour cream

Coat veal lightly with flour, salt and pepper. Heat oil in skillet and brown veal; add onions and cook until just tender. Stir in paprika. Add chicken bouillon, cover and simmer gently 20 minutes until veal is tender. Just before serving, stir in the sour cream and heat through. Do not boil. Serve with noodles. Makes 4 servings.

Beef Stroganoff

2 to 2½ pounds beef (tenderloin, sirloin or flank steak)
3 tablespoons flour
½ teaspoon salt
¼ teaspoon pepper
3 tablespoons fat
3 onions, sliced thin
½ cup tomato juice
1 can consomme
½ teaspoon sugar
½ cup sour cream
½ pound sliced mushrooms
3 tablespoons Burgundy wine (optional)

Cut meat in thin strips. Toss in flour, salt and pepper. Brown meat and onions in 3 tablespoons hot fat. Add tomato juice, consommé and sugar. Reduce heat and simmer until meat is tender. Blend in sour cream, mushrooms and wine. Heat but do not boil. Serve over buttered noodles, rice or mashed potatoes. Makes 4 to 6 servings.

Salmon Diable

½ cup sour cream
¼ cup mayonnaise
¼ cup sherry
1 tablespoon lemon juice
1 tablespoon Worcestershire sauce
½ teaspoon dry mustard
2 eggs, slightly beaten
⅛ teaspoon Tabasco
¼ cup chopped celery (optional)
1 1-pound can salmon, drained and flaked
⅓ cup cracker crumbs
¼ cup snipped parsley
1 tablespoon snipped chives, fresh or frozen
Salt and pepper to taste
Paprika
Lemon slices

Mix together sour cream, mayonnaise, sherry, lemon juice, Worcestershire sauce, mustard, celery, eggs and Tabasco. Pour over the salmon, cracker crumbs, parsley, chives, salt and pepper. Stir gently until well blended. Spoon into 6 baking shells or a baking dish. Sprinkle with paprika and bake in a preheated 350° oven for 30 minutes. Garnish with lemon slices. Serve with the following sauce. Serves 4.

Sauce

1 cup sour cream
1 teaspoon mustard
1 teaspoon horseradish
¼ teaspoon salt
1 tablespoon snipped chives

Combine and stir.

Chicken Almond

3 cups cooked chicken
3 tablespoons oil
2 cups celery, cut in ½-inch slices
2¼ cups chicken stock
3 tablespoons soy sauce
4 tablespoons cornstarch
1 teaspoon sugar
½ cup water
2 16-ounce cans Chinese vegetables
½ cup whole almonds
2 tablespoons sherry
1 or 2 packages frozen Chinese pea pods, thawed, drained and dried (optional)

Heat chicken in hot oil until golden brown. Add celery, chicken stock and soy sauce. Cook a few minutes. Mix together cornstarch, sugar and water. Add to chicken mixture and simmer until thickened. Add Chinese vegetables, almonds and sherry. Simmer just until mixture is heated through. If desired, add pea pods and stir into hot mixture. Do not overcook. Serve over Chinese noodles or rice. Serves 6 to 8.

Barbecued Beef Strips

2 pounds round steak (cut ½- to ¾-inch thick)
2 tablespoons oil
2 cups tomato sauce
⅓ cup water
2 tablespoons brown sugar
1 tablespoon prepared mustard
1 tablespoon Worcestershire sauce
1 medium onion, thinly sliced

Slice round steak in strips ⅛-inch thick or thinner and 3 to 4 inches long. Brown strips in oil. Pour off drippings. Combine tomato sauce, water, brown sugar, mustard and Worcestershire sauce. Add sauce and onion. Stir. Cover and simmer for 30 minutes or until meat is tender. Serves 6 to 8.

Baked Ham and Chicken

3 cooked chicken breasts, cubed
3 smoked pork chops, cubed
1 10-ounce can cream of celery soup
½ soup can milk
½ soup can sherry
½ cup chopped pimiento
1 green pepper, chopped
½ cup grated Parmesan cheese

Arrange chicken and chops in casserole. Mix together soup, milk, sherry, pimiento and green pepper. Pour over meat; sprinkle with cheese and bake in a 350° oven for 30 minutes. Makes 4 servings.

Company Entrees in 60 Minutes or Less!

We've put together a delicious variety of extra-special company entrées that can be prepared in 60 minutes or less! Some are elegant in their simplicity, such as Roast Beef Tenderloin. Still others will earn you rave reviews by merely using leftovers. Try the Egg Casserole—it's fabulous for a brunch along with sliced fresh fruit and wedges of oven-toasted French bread. Relax and enjoy your company instead of staying in your kitchen.

Turkey Tetrazzini

- ¾ cup butter or margarine
- ¾ cup flour
- 3 teaspoons salt
- ⅛ teaspoon nutmeg
- 4 cups milk
- 2 cups turkey or chicken stock
- 4 egg yolks
- 1 cup milk
- ½ cup dry sherry
- 1 pound thin spaghetti
- 6 cups leftover turkey or chicken (cut in 1½-inch pieces)
- ½ pound mushrooms, sliced
- 1 tablespoon butter
- 2 cups grated Swiss cheese
- ¼ cup grated Parmesan cheese

Melt ¾ cup butter in a large saucepan. Remove from heat and stir in flour, salt and nutmeg. Gradually add 4 cups milk and stock and bring to a boil, stirring constantly. Boil 2 minutes or until slightly thickened. In a small bowl, beat egg yolks with remaining milk. Pour 2 tablespoons hot mixture into yolks and then pour yolk mixture into saucepan, beating constantly until sauce is hot. Do not boil. Remove from heat and stir in sherry. Cook spaghetti as directed on package and drain. Return spaghetti to kettle and toss lightly with 2 cups sauce. Divide spaghetti in half and place in two 12 x 8 x 2-inch baking dishes. Sauté mushrooms in remaining butter. Add mushrooms and turkey to 2 cups of the sauce. Reserve remaining sauce. Spoon half of turkey mixture to center of each dish; sprinkle with Swiss cheese. Cover with foil and refrigerate 1 hour or overnight. One hour before serving, place in a preheated 350° oven for 45 minutes. Uncover and sprinkle with Parmesan cheese, broil 2 minutes. Heat reserved sauce and serve with casserole.

Note: Casserole can be frozen. Let thaw 1 hour and bake, covered, in a preheated 350° oven 60 minutes until bubbly. Serves 12.

Chicken Della Robbia

- 2 to 3 fryers, cut up
- 4 tablespoons butter
- 2 tablespoons vegetable oil
- 2 onions, sliced
- 1¼ cups water
- ½ teaspoon instant chicken bouillon
- ½ pound mushrooms, sliced
- 1 cup white raisins
- 2 teaspoons salt
- ¼ cup lemon juice
- 1 clove garlic, minced
- ½ teaspoon ground cloves
- ½ teaspoon allspice
- ½ teaspoon ginger
- ¼ cup brown sugar
- 1 cup walnut halves
- ½ cup water
- 1 tablespoon cornstarch
- 2 cups green seedless grapes
- 2 cups orange sections
- 12 cherries

In a large Dutch oven or fryer, sauté chicken pieces in butter and oil until golden brown. Add onions and sauté. Combine 1¼ cup water with ½ teaspoon instant chicken bouillon. Add with mushrooms, raisins, salt, lemon juice, garlic, spices and brown sugar. Simmer, covered, turning 1 or 2 times, for 35 minutes or until tender. Add walnut halves. Push chicken to side of pan. Blend cornstarch with ½ cup water and stir into pan liquid. Heat until smooth and thickened. Add grapes, oranges and cherries and heat through for 2 to 3 minutes. Serve at once on heated platter or in a chafing dish. Serves 8 to 12.

Steak Diane

4 tenderloin or rib-eye steaks,
(¼- to ½-inch thick)
4 tablespoons butter
4 tablespoons snipped chives
4 tablespoons snipped parsley
1 teaspoon Dijon mustard
1 teaspoon Worcestershire sauce
¼ teaspoon salt
¼ teaspoon pepper
½ cup dry vermouth
¼ cup brandy

In a large chafing dish or electric frying pan, melt 2 tablespoons of the butter and brown steaks quickly, turning once. Remove to platter. Add remaining butter, chives, parsley, mustard, Worcestershire sauce, salt and pepper and bring to a light boil. Add vermouth and simmer, stirring occasionally for 2 to 3 minutes. Heat brandy in a small saucepan (do not boil). Return steaks to skillet. Pour heated brandy over steaks and flame. Serve as soon as flame dies, spooning sauce over the steaks. Serves 4.

Sole and Shrimp au Gratin

2 pounds fillet of sole
½ teaspoon salt
¼ cup dry sherry
2 tablespoons lemon juice
2 tablespoons butter or margarine
2 tablespoons flour
Dash Tabasco sauce
1 teaspoon instant chicken bouillon
½ cup light cream
½ cup grated Parmesan cheese
12 to 16 ounces shrimp, cooked and cleaned
Snipped parsley

Arrange fillets in baking dish and sprinkle with salt. Combine sherry and lemon juice and pour over fish. Bake in a preheated 350° oven for 15 minutes. Drain juices and reserve. Return fish to oven and bake for another 10 minutes or until it flakes easily with fork. While it bakes, add enough water to the reserved broth to make 1 cup. Melt butter in saucepan over low heat. Stir in flour, Tabasco, broth and bouillon. Cook over low heat, stirring, until sauce is smooth and bubbly. Remove from heat; stir in cream. Heat just to boiling, stirring constantly. Add cheese and shrimp and stir until cheese is melted. Alternate layers of fish and sauce in a chafing dish, ending with sauce. Garnish with parsley. Serves 6.

Veal Vermouth

1½ pounds thin veal steak
2 tablespoons flour
¼ cup butter
1 clove garlic, minced
½ pound mushrooms, sliced
½ teaspoon salt
Dash of pepper
1 tablespoon lemon juice
⅓ cup dry vermouth
2 tablespoons snipped parsley

Flatten veal to ¼-inch thick. Cut into 2-inch squares and dredge in flour. Melt butter and sauté veal, a little at a time, until golden brown on both sides. Return all meat and the garlic to the skillet and heap mushrooms on top. Sprinkle with salt, pepper and lemon juice. Pour on vermouth, cover and cook over low heat for 20 minutes or until veal is fork tender. Add more vermouth if additional liquid is needed. Sprinkle with parsley just before serving. Serves 4.

Chicken with Polynesian Vegetables

2 frying chickens, cut up
2 tablespoons butter
Flour, seasoned with salt and pepper

Coat chicken lightly with seasoned flour. Melt butter in a shallow baking dish. Arrange chicken in a dish. Bake, uncovered at 400° 20 minutes. Turn chicken, reduce heat to 350° and bake for 30 to 35 additional minutes, or until chicken is tender. Serves 6.

Polynesian Vegetables

1 cup water
1 teaspoon instant beef bouillon
1 tablespoon soy sauce
½ teaspoon ginger
2 cups diagonally sliced celery
2 cups diagonally sliced carrot
2 cups green pepper, cut into 1-inch pieces
1 cup sliced green onion
1 5-ounce can water chestnuts, thinly sliced
½ cup unsweetened pineapple juice
2 to 3 teaspoons cornstarch

Combine first 4 ingredients in a saucepan. Bring to a boil. Reduce heat; add celery, carrot and green pepper. Return to boiling; cover and simmer 5 minutes. Add green onion and water chestnuts. Cook 2 minutes. Remove vegetables to heated dish and keep warm. Combine cornstarch and pineapple juice. Stir into broth and cook, stirring until thickened. Pour over vegetables.

Fillet of Sole Florentine

2 pounds sole or turbot fillets
2 tablespoons butter or margarine, cut into dots
½ teaspoon salt
2 10-ounce packages frozen, chopped spinach, cooked and drained
1 can cream of mushroom soup
3 tablespoons sherry
1 tablespoon butter or margarine, melted
3 tablespoons dry bread crumbs
2 tablespoons grated Parmesan cheese

Wash, drain and dry the fish fillets. Arrange in a baking dish and dot with the butter. Sprinkle with salt, cover the dish and bake in a preheated 350° oven for 15 minutes. Remove from oven and drain liquid. Spread spinach over the top of the fish. Blend soup with sherry and pour over all. Mix bread crumbs with melted butter and cheese and sprinkle over top. Bake uncovered for 20 minutes. Yield: 6 to 8 servings.

Spanakopitta (Spinach Pie)

2 packages frozen, chopped spinach
2 tablespoons butter
1 small onion, chopped
¼ cup chopped scallions
2 tablespoons parsley
1 teaspoon dill
1 teaspoon salt
¼ teaspoon pepper
¼ cup milk
3 eggs
¼ pound feta cheese
½ pound phylo pastry
1 cup melted butter

Thaw spinach and drain. Sauté onion in 2 tablespoons butter. Add scallions and cook until they wilt. Add spinach and seasonings. Toss lightly. Remove from heat and add milk. Beat eggs lightly in another bowl and add feta cheese, coarsely crumbled. Add to spinach mixture, mix well. With a pastry brush, coat bottom and sides of an 11 x 7 x 2-inch baking dish with melted butter. Line with 8 sheets of phylo, brushing each sheet with melted butter. Pour in spinach mixture and fold excess pastry back over filling. Top with 8 sheets of phylo, brushing each sheet with butter. Trim overlap. Brush with butter and score into diamonds. Bake in a 350° oven 45 minutes. Let stand 10 minutes before serving. Serves 4.

Quiche Lorraine au Fromage with Foolproof Crust

1 9-inch pie shell
1 cup grated Swiss cheese
4 eggs
1½ cups milk or light cream
¼ teaspoon salt
⅛ teaspoon pepper
⅛ teaspoon nutmeg
2 tablespoons butter, cut into dots

Optional Variations

1 onion, sliced and sautéed
¼ pound sliced, sautéed mushrooms
4 to 6 slices crisp, cooked bacon (or bacon substitute)
8 ounces small cooked shrimp
7 ounces crabmeat, flaked
1 package drained, chopped spinach

Spread cheese and/or optional variations in Foolproof Crust. Lightly beat eggs and milk. Add salt, pepper and nutmeg and pour into pie shell. Distribute butter dots over top. Bake in a preheated 375° oven 35 to 40 minutes or until a knife inserted in center comes out clean. Allow to stand 10 minutes before cutting. Serves 4 to 6.

Foolproof Crust

¼ pound butter or margarine, softened
1 cup flour
¼ teaspoon salt

Cut flour and salt into butter and mix until a ball forms. Pat dough with hands into a 9-inch pie plate, mending if necessary and fluting edge if desired. Prick generously with a fork and bake at 400° for 7 minutes.

Roast Beef Tenderloin

1 4- to 4½-pound beef tenderloin
½ cup oil
½ cup Burgundy wine
2 tablespoons grated onion
1 clove garlic, minced
1½ teaspoons salt
5 drops Tabasco (optional)

Combine all ingredients and allow beef to marinate in refrigerator at least 2 hours. Remove from sauce. Preheat oven to 450°. Place meat in a shallow pan and brush with marinade. Bake for 15 minutes. Reduce temperature to 350°. Baste with marinade occasionally and continue baking for 35 minutes for medium rare, or less time for rare. Makes 6 servings.

Last Minute Additions for Memorable Meals

In Last Minute Additions for Memorable Meals, we've included some outstanding selections for your dining pleasure . . . appetizers, quick breads, desserts and beverages. Any menu is sure to be enhanced by one of our quick and easy recipes.

Appetizers

Spring Garden Dip

½ cup small curd cottage cheese
1 tablespoon finely grated carrot
2 teaspoons freeze-dried chives
1 teaspoon finely grated green pepper
½ teaspoon seasoned salt
Dash garlic powder
⅛ teaspoon dry mustard
Dash white pepper
1 cup plain yogurt

In small mixing bowl beat cottage cheese; blend in carrot, chives, green pepper, salt, garlic powder, mustard and pepper. Beat until fairly smooth. Fold in yogurt. Cover; chill. Use as dip for chips or assorted raw vegetables. Serve in hollowed-out center of a cabbage head. 1½ cups.

Aloha Dip

12 macaroons, crushed in small pieces
¼ cup firmly packed light brown sugar
1 pint dairy sour cream
1 large pineapple
Assorted berries
Seedless green grapes
Peaches, sliced

Mix together macaroons, sugar and sour cream. Chill several hours to soften macaroon crumbs. Do not stir again or macaroon crumbs will break into small pieces. Slice a cap-shaped piece off top of pineapple, about 1 inch below bottom of leaves. Hollow out center of pineapple with a sharp knife. Leave a firm shell to put the macaroon sauce into. Cut fruit into small pieces, discarding hard core that runs down the center. Fill pineapple shell with dip. Replace pineapple top if you like. Place in center of large platter. Arrange pineapple chunks, assorted berries, grapes and peaches in groups around pineapple. If you like, sprinkle fruit with kirsch or brandy. Yield: 1 quart.

Guacamole

1 cup mashed avocado
1 tablespoon lemon juice
1 teaspoon salt
1½ teaspoons grated onion

Note: For variety, add 1 or more of the following:

Dash of Tabasco
1 teaspoon curry powder
1 teaspoon Worcestershire sauce
½ teaspoon chili powder

Combine all ingredients and mix well. Chill several hours. Serve with chips or crackers. Makes 1 cup Guacamole.

Dippers

Scallions
Green Beans
Carrot or celery sticks
Fresh pineapple spears
Radishes
Green pepper slices
Cucumber or zucchini rounds
Cauliflowerets
Mushrooms
Kohlrabi slices
Turnip slices
Asparagus spears

Serve an assortment of these vegetables and fruits with the usual chips, pretzel sticks, and crackers.

Sherried Hot Crab

1 8-ounce package cream cheese
1 tablespoon mayonnaise
2 tablespoons dry sherry
1 teaspoon lemon juice
Dash Tabasco
1 7½-ounce can crab meat, remove cartilage and drain
⅓ cup sliced unblanched almonds

Mix together all ingredients except crab meat and almonds until smooth. Stir in crab meat. Spoon into shallow baking dish. Top with almonds and bake in a preheated 350° oven for 15 to 20 minutes until hot and bubbly. Serve with crackers. Serves 4 to 6.

Antipasto

1 7-ounce can white tuna
½ pound cooked shrimp or 1 can shrimp
1 jar chili sauce
½ cup catsup
1 4-ounce jar stuffed olives
1 2-ounce jar button mushrooms
1 16-ounce jar sweet mixed pickles
1 carrot, thinly sliced

Combine all ingredients and chill for at least 30 minutes. Serve with crackers or in ramekins with cocktail forks. Serves 4 to 6.

Marinated Mushrooms

1 pound small mushrooms, cleaned and dried
½ cup olive oil
2 tablespoons lemon juice
2 tablespoons vinegar
1 teaspoon salt
½ teaspoon freshly ground pepper
¼ teaspoon thyme
1 teaspoon tarragon

Combine all ingredients and simmer over low heat for 5 to 10 minutes. Cool; refrigerate in marinade overnight. Bring to room temperature before serving. Yield: 32 to 38.

Broiled Ground Beef Triangles

4 to 5 slices of bread, toasted on 1 side
Softened butter
Prepared mustard
½ pound ground round
¼ cup milk
½ teaspoon salt
½ teaspoon pepper
1 tablespoon instant minced onion

Spread untoasted side of bread with butter and then lightly with mustard. Combine meat, milk, salt, pepper, and onion. Spread on top of mustard to the edges of bread. Broil, meat side up, 5 to 7 minutes until meat is done. Cut each sandwich into 4 triangles. Makes 16 to 20 triangles.

Crab Meat Puff

1 6-ounce can crab meat
1 3-ounce package cream cheese, softened
¼ cup mayonnaise
1 teaspoon minced onion
1 teaspoon salt
⅛ teaspoon pepper
1 tablespoon snipped parsley
Toast rounds

Combine all ingredients except toast rounds. Mound crab meat mixture on toast; broil until bubbly. Makes about 1 cup.

Cheddar in Port

2 tablespoons butter or margarine
1 teaspoon dry mustard
Dash cayenne
½ pound Cheddar cheese, grated
5 tablespoons port wine

Cream butter with mustard and cayenne. Stir in finely grated cheese and wine. Blend thoroughly. Makes 1¼ cups.

Deviled Ham Puffs

2 cups diced ham (¾ pound)
2 tablespoons mayonnaise (more if desired)
2 teaspoons Dijon mustard
1 to 2 teaspoons horseradish
1 teaspoon grated onion

Blend ham in food processor or blender until smooth paste is formed. Add remaining ingredients and process until well blended. Spread on toasted bread rounds and broil until bubbly. Makes 2½ to 3 dozen.

Appetizer Delights

½ cup chopped ripe olives
¼ cup minced green onion
1 cup grated American cheese
¼ cup mayonnaise
1½ teaspoons curry powder (optional)
¼ teaspoon salt
Bread or English muffins, split and toasted

Combine all ingredients except muffins and mix thoroughly. Spread on bread or muffin halves and broil until hot and cheese is melted. Cut in squares or triangles to serve.

Cheese Tarts

Crustades

24 slices of thin bread, crusts trimmed
Softened butter

Roll out bread slice to flatten slightly. Cut bread into 2½-inch rounds and butter both sides. Ease circle into miniature muffin tins so that edges ruffle. Place filling in center and bake in a 325° oven for 15 to 18 minutes until golden brown. Serve warm.

Fillings

24 cubes of Cheddar, Muenster, Swiss or blue cheese
24 teaspoons of clam spread
24 teaspoons of cream cheese, olive spread
24 teaspoons of ham spread

Crustades may also be baked empty and filled with cold spread, such as chicken, ham, shrimp, or egg salad.

Quick Breads

Applesauce and Raisin Bread

> 2 cups flour
> 1 tablespoon baking powder
> 1 teaspoon salt
> 1 teaspoon cinnamon
> ½ teaspoon ground cloves
> 1 cup unsweetened applesauce
> 2 eggs, beaten
> ¼ cup dark brown sugar, firmly packed
> ¼ cup vegetable oil
> 1 cup seedless raisins
> ½ cup finely chopped nuts (optional)

Stir together flour, baking powder, salt, cinnamon and cloves. Combine applesauce, eggs, sugar and oil; stir in raisins and nuts. Add all at once to flour, stirring only until flour is moistened. Pour into greased 8½ x 4½-inch loaf pan. Bake in a 350° oven 50 to 55 minutes or until done. Allow to cool in pan 15 minutes before removing. Makes 1 loaf.

Irish Soda Bread

> 2 cups flour
> 1 tablespoon sugar
> 1½ teaspoons baking powder
> 1 teaspoon baking soda
> ¼ teaspoon salt
> ¼ cup butter or margarine, softened
> ¾ cup raisins
> 1½ teaspoons caraway seed (optional)
> 1 cup buttermilk
> 1 egg, slightly beaten with 1 tablespoon water

Sift flour, sugar, baking powder, soda and salt into a large mixing bowl. Cut in butter with a pastry blender until mixture resembles coarse meal. Stir in raisins and caraway seed. Add buttermilk, blending to moisten the dry ingredients. Turn dough onto a floured board; knead for several minutes until smooth. Form dough into a round ball and place on a greased baking sheet. Flatten ball until dough is about 1½ inches high; brush top and sides with egg-water mixture. Cut a ½-inch deep cross in top of bread with sharp knife. Bake in a 375° oven 30 to 40 minutes or until a wooden pick inserted in center comes out clean. Transfer to wire rack to cool; brush top with butter or margarine and cover with cloth. Yield: 1 loaf.

Blueberry Corn Muffins

> 1 8½-ounce package corn muffin mix
> 1 tablespoon brown sugar
> 1 egg
> ⅓ cup milk
> ½ cup blueberries (canned, drained, fresh or frozen and thawed)

Blend muffin mix, sugar, egg and milk. Batter should be slightly lumpy. Stir in blueberries. Fill greased muffin cups half full. Bake in a preheated 400° oven 15 to 20 minutes until golden brown. Makes 8 to 12 muffins, depending on size.

Biscuits

> 2 cups flour
> 1 tablespoon baking powder
> 1 teaspoon salt
> ¼ cup shortening
> ½ to ¾ cup milk

Stir together dry ingredients. Cut in shortening until mixture resembles coarse crumbs. Blend in enough milk to make a soft dough. Turn onto lightly floured surface and knead gently 30 seconds. Roll out ½-inch thick and cut biscuits with a floured cutter. Place on ungreased baking sheet and bake in a 450° oven 10 to 12 minutes, or until lightly browned. Makes 12 biscuits.

Pumpkin Walnut Bread

> 2 cups flour
> 2 teaspoons baking powder
> ½ teaspoon baking soda
> 1 teaspoon salt
> 1 teaspoon ground cinnamon
> ½ teaspoon ground nutmeg
> 2 eggs
> 1 cup solid-pack pumpkin
> 1 cup sugar
> ½ cup milk
> ¼ cup melted butter
> 1 cup chopped walnuts

Sift together first 6 ingredients. Beat eggs slightly in a bowl; stir in pumpkin, sugar, milk and melted butter, mixing well. Add dry ingredients and mix well. Stir in nuts. Spread in a well-greased 9 x 5 x 3-inch loaf pan. Bake in a 350° oven 50 to 55 minutes, or until edges begin to pull away from sides of pan and wooden pick inserted in center comes out clean. Cool in pan on wire rack for 5 minutes, then remove loaf from pan and cool completely. Makes 1 loaf.

Desserts

Lemon Velvet

2½ cups graham cracker crumbs
⅔ cup margarine, melted
2 8-ounce packages cream cheese, softened
1 cup sugar
2 tablespoons milk
2 tablespoons grated lemon rind
1 cup chopped walnuts
2 cups whipping cream, whipped
Lemon slices
Graham cracker crumbs

Combine 2½ cups crumbs and margarine. Press onto bottom of 13 x 9-inch pan. In mixing bowl, combine cream cheese, sugar, milk and lemon rind; mix until smooth. Fold in nuts and whipped cream. Spread mixture over crust. Freeze. Cut into squares. Garnish with lemon slices and graham cracker crumbs. 16 to 20 servings.

Coconut-Strawberry Torte

1 10-ounce package frozen strawberries
2 envelopes unflavored gelatin
1 cup sugar
¼ teaspoon salt
2 eggs, separated
3 8-ounce packages cream cheese, room temperature
Red food coloring
1 cup heavy cream, whipped
1 cup flaked coconut
Fresh strawberries, sliced

Drain syrup from strawberries and set aside. In top of double boiler combine gelatin, ¾ cup sugar and salt. Beat together strawberry syrup and egg yolks and add to gelatin mixture. Heat over simmering water 10 minutes. Cool to room temperature and add thawed strawberries. Stir. Whip cheese until fluffy. Beat in strawberry mixture and food coloring. Chill. Stir occasionally until mixture mounds when dropped from a spoon. Beat egg whites until stiff but not dry. Fold into gelatin. Fold in whipped cream. Pour into a 9-inch round springform pan. Sprinkle with half the coconut. Chill several hours. When ready to serve, run knife dipped in hot water around the edge of pan. Release spring and remove from pan. Press remaining coconut into sides and top of cake. Garnish with sliced strawberries. Serves 14.

Kahlua Dessert

4 scoops vanilla ice cream
2 cups coconut, toasted
2 ounces Kahlua

Roll scoops of ice cream in toasted coconut. Pour Kahlua over the top. Brandy or Creme de Cacao may also be used. Serves 2.

Batter-up Brownies

1 cup all-purpose flour
½ teaspoon baking powder
½ teaspoon salt
½ cup shortening
1½ cups sugar
3 eggs
½ cup peanut butter
1 teaspoon vanilla
1 cup chopped peanuts
1 6-ounce package chocolate chips

Mix together flour, baking powder and salt. Melt shortening. Remove from heat and cool slightly. Add remaining ingredients in order listed. Mix thoroughly. Spread in well-greased 13 x 9 x 2-inch pan. Bake in pre-heated 350° oven 25 to 30 minutes. Cool in pan. Cut into squares. About 2 dozen.

Treasure Toffee Cake

¼ cup sugar
1 teaspoon cinnamon
2 cups flour
1 cup sugar
1½ teaspoons baking powder
1 teaspoon baking soda
¼ teaspoon salt
1 teaspoon vanilla
1 cup sour cream
½ cup butter, softened
2 eggs
¼ cup chopped nuts
3 1⅛-ounce chocolate toffee bars, coarsely crushed
¼ cup melted butter
Confectioners' sugar

Combine cinnamon and ¼ cup sugar. Combine remaining ingredients except nuts, candy and melted butter. Blend at low speed until moistened. Beat at medium speed 3 minutes. Spoon half of the batter into greased and floured 10-inch bundt pan. Sprinkle with 2 tablespoons cinnamon-sugar mixture. Spoon remaining batter into pan. Top with remaining cinnamon-sugar mixture, nuts and candy. Pour melted butter over top. Bake in a 325° oven 45 minutes. Cool 15 minutes. Remove from pan; dust with confectioners' sugar. Serves 16.

Texas Chocolate Cake

2 cups cake flour or 1¾ cups all-purpose flour
2 cups sugar
½ teaspoon salt
1 teaspoon baking soda
2 eggs
½ cup sour cream
2 tablespoons butter
1 cup water
4 tablespoons cocoa

Combine flour, sugar, salt, baking soda, eggs, and sour cream. In a small saucepan bring butter, water, and cocoa to a boil. Add to flour mixture; mix well and pour in greased 9 x 13 x 2-inch oblong pan. Bake 20 minutes at 350°.

Icing

1 pound confectioners' sugar
1 teaspoon vanilla
1 cup chopped walnuts
1 tablespoon butter
6 tablespoons milk
4 tablespoons cocoa

Combine confectioners' sugar, vanilla and walnuts. Bring butter, milk, and cocoa to a boil. Add at once to sugar mixture. Mix thoroughly. Ice cake while hot.

Peppermint and Ice Cream Cake

¾ cup round hard peppermint candies
¼ cup water
2 cups heavy cream, whipped
¼ cup confectioners' sugar
½ teaspoon vanilla
1 angel food cake
1 pint vanilla ice cream

In blender container, blend ½ cup candies on high speed until coarsely crushed. Remove to waxed paper. Blend remaining ¼ cup candies but leave in the blender. Add water; blend until syrupy. In small bowl beat cream, sugar and vanilla at medium speed until stiff peaks form. Slice cake into 3 layers. Sprinkle bottom layer with 2 tablespoons peppermint syrup. Spread ½ cup whipped cream over the cake; sprinkle with 1 tablespoon crushed candies. Top with second cake layer and repeat the step above. Invert top layer. Sprinkle cut side with remaining syrup. Place right side up on the cake. Spread remaining cream on top and sides of cake, dusting sides with crushed candies.

Scoop ice cream into balls. Place ice cream balls on top of cake. Sprinkle with crushed candies. Freeze until served. Serves 10.

Walnut Shortbread

1 cup butter
1 cup margarine
1 cup sugar
1 cup chopped walnuts
1 teaspoon vanilla
4 cups sifted flour

Cream butter and margarine; add sugar and beat until light and fluffy. Beat nuts and vanilla into mixture. Add flour and mix well. Pat dough into a 15½ x 10½ x 1-inch jelly roll pan, smoothing out to fill the pan. Bake in a preheated 325° oven for 40 to 45 minutes or until golden. Cool in pan and then cut into bars. Makes seventy-five 2-inch bars.

Cereal 'N' Chocolate Chip Cookies

1¾ cups flour
1 teaspoon baking soda
½ teaspoon salt
1 cup butter or margarine
¾ cup granulated sugar
¾ cup brown sugar
2 eggs
1 teaspoon vanilla
2 cups oven-toasted rice cereal
1 6-ounce package semisweet chocolate chips

Stir together flour, soda and salt. Set aside. Cream together butter and sugars. Add egg and vanilla and beat well. Stir in dry ingredients. Add rice cereal and chocolate chips. Drop by level tablespoons onto greased baking sheets. Bake in 350° oven about 10 minutes or until lightly browned. Cool on baking sheet 1 minute. Place on wire racks. Makes about 6 dozen 2½-inch cookies.

Peanut Butter Cookies

Mix ¾ cup peanut butter into butter-sugar mixture.

Chocolate Chip Raisin Cookies

Add 1 cup seedless raisins with the chocolate chips.

Holiday Fruit Cookies

In place of chocolate chips, use 1 cup finely cut, mixed candied fruit.

Beverages

Spiced Ice Tea

- 1 cup sugar
- 1 cup water
- 1 whole nutmeg
- 2 sticks cinnamon
- 1 orange
- 12 cloves
- 2 cups orange juice
- ¼ cup lemon juice
- 3 cups double-strength iced tea

Put sugar, water, nutmeg and cinnamon in a saucepan. Simmer 10 minutes. Stud orange with whole cloves and add to mixture. Cover. Cool and strain. Add the orange juice, lemon juice and iced tea. Serve over ice cubes in tall glasses. Serves 12.

Café Brulot

- 1 cup brandy
- Peel of 1 orange
- 6 whole cloves
- 4 whole allspice
- 4 cinnamon sticks
- 3 tablespoons sugar
- 3 cups hot double-strength coffee

In chafing dish, over direct heat, combine all ingredients except coffee. Heat until hot. Carefully ignite brandy with a long match. Let it flame for 1 to 2 minutes. Slowly pour coffee into flaming brandy. Ladle into café brulot cups or demitasse cups. Serves 8.

Mulled Wine Punch

- 2½ cups sugar
- 1¼ cups water
- 4 dozen whole cloves
- 6 cinnamon sticks
- 3 crushed nutmegs
- Peel of 3 lemons and 2 oranges
- 3 cups hot lemon or lime juice
- 3 bottles red wine
- 12 lemon slices
- 12 pineapple chunks

Make a syrup by boiling water, sugar, cloves, cinnamon, nutmeg and peels. Strain. Add hot juice to the strained mix. Heat this well and add wine. Serve very hot in coffee cups or mugs with a slice of lemon and a chunk of pineapple in each cup. Serves 16.

Apple Cider Punch

- 4 cups apple cider
- 2 cups cranberry juice
- 1 cup orange juice
- 1 12-ounce can apricot nectar
- 1 cup sugar
- 2 sticks cinnamon

Heat and let simmer 20 minutes. Top punch bowl with floating orange slices decorated with cloves. Serves 20 to 25.

Sparkling Ruby Punch

Sherbet Ring

- 1 pint raspberry sherbet
- 1 pint lemon sherbet
- Mint leaves
- 2 cups cranberry-apple juice, chilled

Using small ice cream scoop, form 4 scoops each of raspberry and lemon sherbet. Freeze. Arrange leaves in bottom of 4½-cup ring mold. Place balls of sherbet alternately in mold. Pour in 1 cup cranberry-apple juice; freeze. Add remaining juice; freeze firm.

Punch

- 1 46-ounce can pineapple juice
- 2 6-ounce cans frozen lemonade concentrate
- 4 cups cranberry-apple juice
- 1 8-ounce jar maraschino cherries
- 2 oranges, sliced
- Red food coloring
- 1 quart ginger ale or sparkling water, chilled

In a large bowl combine pineapple juice, lemonade, cranberry-apple juice, cherries with syrup and sliced oranges. Add food coloring to desired color. Chill. To serve: Combine punch and ginger ale in punch bowl. Unmold sherbet ring in warm water; float in fruit punch. Yield: 3 quarts.

Cocoa

- ¼ cup cocoa
- 4 tablespoons sugar
- Pinch salt
- Pinch cinnamon
- 1 cup water
- 3 cups milk
- Marshmallow
- Whipped cream

Combine dry ingredients in a small saucepan and add water gradually, stirring well. Cook over low heat for 3 to 4 minutes. Slowly add milk and heat until steaming hot. Serve with marshmallow or a dollop of whipped cream. Serves 4.

Dinner is ready in a matter of minutes if you are fortunate enough to have a microwave oven. In general, cooking time in a microwave takes about one quarter of the time it does in a conventional oven. Some models can be programmed to begin your meal while you are away from home. Cleanup is just a quick swish of a paper towel. Leftovers can be reheated in a snap. The following recipes are among the best in creative alternatives to conventional cooking. The power setting is indicated in parentheses following the recipe.

Appetizers

Appetizer Meatballs (High)

1 pound ground chuck
1 onion, finely chopped
¾ teaspoon salt
1 10½-ounce can tomato soup
3 tablespoons lemon juice
¼ cup brown sugar
1 1-pound can pineapple chunks, drained

Form 1-inch balls from ground chuck. In a 9-inch square dish, combine onion, salt, soup, lemon juice and brown sugar. Cover and microwave 7 minutes, stirring twice. Add meatballs to sauce. Microwave 5 to 6 minutes, covered, stirring twice. Add pineapple; heat 1 minute. Serves 6.

Delightful Crab Dip (High)

1 8-ounce package softened cream cheese
⅓ cup mayonnaise
1 teaspoon creamy horseradish
1½ tablespoons minced onion
½ teaspoon seasoned salt
1 tablespoon chopped parsley
Dash garlic powder
1 6-ounce package chopped crab meat

Blend cream cheese, mayonnaise, horseradish, onion and seasoned salt. Fold in parsley, garlic powder and crab meat. Serve well chilled with fresh vegetables and crackers or serve hot. To heat, place in microwave oven for 1½ minutes. Stir and heat another 1 to 1½ minutes. To soften cream cheese if refrigerator cold, unwrap it from foil, place on a plate and microwave for 30 to 45 seconds.

Soups

Corn and Frank Chowder (High)

3 slices bacon, chopped
5 frankfurters, sliced
1 onion, chopped
4 potatoes, diced
1 cup water
2 teaspoons salt
¼ teaspoon pepper
½ teaspoon basil
1 can creamed corn
1 5-ounce can evaporated milk

In a 2½-quart dish, microwave bacon 2½ minutes. Add franks and onion; microwave 4 minutes, stirring after 2 minutes. Add potatoes and water. Microwave 12 minutes; stir after 6 minutes. Add remaining ingredients and microwave 4 minutes. Serves 4 to 6.

Vegetable Soup (High)

3 slices raw bacon, diced
¼ cup chopped onion
1 cup chopped celery
1 cup thinly sliced carrots
1 cup potatoes, in ¼-inch cubes
3 tablespoons flour
3 cups tomato juice
1 cup water
½ teaspoon thyme
1 cube beef bouillon, crumbled
Salt and pepper
1 8-ounce can peas and carrots

Place onion and bacon in 2½-quart bowl. Cover and microwave 3 minutes, stirring twice. Add celery, carrots and potatoes. Cover and microwave 10 minutes, stirring twice. Add flour, tomato juice, water, thyme, bouillon, salt and pepper. Heat, uncovered, 10 minutes. Add peas and carrots; heat 3 minutes. Let stand 3 minutes. Serves 6.

Enchiladas p. 68

Entrees

Prize-Winning Elegant Chicken (High)

2 10-ounce packages frozen asparagus spears
¼ cup butter
¼ cup blanched, slivered almonds
¼ cup flour
½ teaspoon salt
⅛ teaspoon pepper
1 10½-ounce can chicken and rice soup
1 cup chicken broth
3 cups cooked chicken, cut bite size
Paprika

Slit tops of boxes of asparagus. Microwave 5 minutes, open boxes and rearrange spears, and microwave 5 minutes more. Set aside. Microwave butter in 9-inch pie plate for 30 seconds. Add almonds to butter. Microwave 1½ minutes, stirring every 30 seconds. Mix together flour, salt, pepper and toasted almonds. Add soup and broth, stirring well. Microwave 3 to 5 minutes, stirring every minute, until thick. In a 12 x 8-inch casserole, alternate layers of chicken and asparagus. Cover with butter sauce. Sprinkle with paprika. Cover with plastic wrap and microwave 5 to 6 minutes. Turn dish one-half turn after 2½ minutes. Garnish with almonds. Serves 6 to 8.

Enchiladas (High)

1 medium onion, chopped
1 tablespoon water
1 pound ground round
½ cup shredded Cheddar cheese
½ cup sour cream
2 teaspoons parsley flakes
1 teaspoon seasoned salt
⅛ teaspoon pepper
10 to 12 flour tortillas
1 15-ounce can tomato sauce
½ cup chopped green pepper
2 teaspoons chili powder
½ teaspoon oregano
⅛ teaspoon minced garlic
½ cup water

Combine onion and water in a 1½-quart covered casserole and microwave 2 to 3 minutes. Add crumbled ground round. Microwave 2½ minutes; stir and microwave an additional 2½ minutes. Drain. Add cheese, sour cream, parsley flakes, salt and pepper. Set aside. Wrap tortillas in paper toweling and microwave 1 minute. Combine remaining ingredients. Pour half of this sauce mixture into a 12 x 8-inch dish. Place 2½ tablespoons meat mixture in center of each tortilla. Roll up. Place seam side down in the sauce. Top with remaining sauce. Cover with plastic wrap. Heat 11 to 12 minutes. Turn after 5½ to 6 minutes. Serves 6 to 8.

Barbecued Pork Chops (High)

6 pork chops, ½-inch thick
1 cup barbecue sauce
½ cup chopped onion
⅛ teaspoon minced garlic
½ teaspoon salt
⅛ teaspoon pepper

Arrange chops in a 12 x 8-inch dish. Combine remaining ingredients. Pour over the chops. Cover with plastic wrap and microwave 5 minutes. Let stand covered 5 minutes. Repeat 2 more times, basting with sauce during rest times. If need be, chops can be cooked 5 minutes more after the last standing time. Turn the dish one-quarter turn after each rest period. Serves 4.

Fish Fillets with Mushrooms (High)

3 tablespoons butter
2 green peppers, cut in ½-inch slices
¼ pound thinly sliced fresh mushrooms
1½ pounds fish fillets
Shredded peel of 1 lemon
¼ cup sliced water chestnuts, drained
Salt
Pepper
Paprika

Place green peppers and butter in a 12 x 8-inch dish. Cover with plastic wrap and microwave 3 minutes. Stir after 1½ minutes. Add mushrooms; stir and microwave 5 minutes. Stir after 2½ minutes. Add fish, lemon peel and chestnuts. Spoon sauce over fish. Cover with waxed paper, and microwave 5 to 6 minutes. Stir after 3 minutes. Season, if desired, with salt, pepper and paprika. Serve over cooked rice. Serves 4.

Vegetable and Fish Sauce (High)

2 cups sliced fresh mushrooms
¼ cup sliced fresh green onion
1 tablespoon flour
¼ teaspoon salt
1 tablespoon butter
⅓ cup milk
1 tablespoon prepared mustard
¼ cup sour cream
2 tablespoons dry white wine

In a 1-quart casserole combine mushrooms and onion; sprinkle with flour and salt. Toss; add butter. Cover and microwave 3½ minutes. Stir well after 1½ minutes. Stir in milk and mustard. Microwave, uncovered, 3 to 4 minutes, stirring every 30 seconds. Mix wine and sour cream. Add to mushrooms; microwave 30 seconds. Makes 2½ cups.

Vegetables

Candied Carrots (High)

```
4 large carrots
⅓ cup butter
½ cup sugar
1 teaspoon salt
⅓ teaspoon cinnamon
1 tablespoon water
```

Scrape carrots and cut into thin strips. Place in a deep 1½-quart casserole; set aside. In a small bowl, combine remaining ingredients. Heat 1 minute; spoon sauce over carrots. Cover and microwave 3½ minutes. Stir and baste with sauce. Microwave an additional 3½ minutes. Heat, uncovered, 3 minutes. Serves 3 to 4.

Scalloped Potatoes (High)

```
4 medium potatoes, pared and thinly sliced
3 tablespoons flour
¾ teaspoon salt
1 cup milk, scalded
2 tablespoons butter
  Paprika
```

Arrange half of the potatoes in a 1½-quart casserole. Combine flour and salt; sprinkle half over the potatoes. Layer remaining potatoes and flour and salt. Pour milk over; dot with butter and sprinkle with paprika. Cover and microwave 11 to 12 minutes. Turn dish after 5½ minutes. Let stand, covered, 5 minutes. Serve hot. Serves 4 to 6.

Cheese 'N' Crumb Tomatoes (High)

```
4 tomatoes
⅓ cup bread crumbs
  Dash pepper
½ teaspoon salt
2 tablespoons grated Parmesan cheese
2 tablespoons butter
```

Cut tomatoes in half crosswise and arrange on serving plate, cut side up. In a small bowl, combine bread crumbs, salt, pepper, Parmesan cheese and butter. Microwave, uncovered, 3 to 4 minutes until brown, stirring frequently. Sprinkle crumb mixture over tomatoes. Microwave, uncovered, 3 to 4 minutes, turning a half turn after 2 minutes. Serves 4.

Quick Breads

Banana Muffins (High)

```
2 cups biscuit mix
⅓ cup sugar
1 teaspoon cinnamon
⅛ teaspoon nutmeg
¾ cup mashed banana
¼ cup buttermilk
1 egg, beaten
1 tablespoon vegetable oil
12 to 26 paper cupcake liners
```

Combine dry ingredients in a bowl. Combine banana, buttermilk, egg and oil in another bowl. Mix with dry ingredients, stirring smooth. Fill each liner half-full. Place in microwave cupcake holder or in custard cups. Microwave 6 at a time in a circle for 2½ minutes, turning one-quarter turn every 30 seconds. Makes 12 to 26 muffins, depending on size of liners.

Desserts

Caramel Apple Squares (High)

Crust

```
½ cup butter
1½ cups flour
¼ cup sugar
1 egg yolk
```

Filling

```
30 caramels
2 tablespoons water
6 medium apples, peeled and sliced
1 tablespoon lemon juice
```

Topping

```
1 cup flour
⅓ cup brown sugar
½ cup butter
  Cinnamon-sugar
```

Microwave ½ cup butter for 45 seconds to melt. Blend into flour, sugar and egg yolk. Press into the bottom of 12 x 8 x 2-inch dish. Microwave 5 to 6 minutes. Turn dish one-half turn after 2½ minutes. Unwrap caramels and place in a dish with water. Microwave 2 to 2½ minutes, stirring twice during cooking process. Arrange apples on crust. Drizzle with lemon juice and caramel mixture. Make topping by combining flour and brown sugar; cut in butter. Sprinkle over apples. Sprinkle top with cinnamon-sugar. Microwave 10 to 12 minutes; cool. Yield: 24.

Looking Good

Looking good is the result of many different things . . . skin care, makeup, exercise, nutrition, and most important, attitude! When you feel good about yourself and make those around you feel good, you usually look your best, too!

The "secrets" of beauty are really just good common sense combined with an interest in maintaining yourself at your beauty potential. But of course it helps to have some information at your fingertips, and so we're providing a few suggestions on skin care, makeup and hair care.

Tips on Skin Care

Three simple steps that take just minutes twice a day and keep your complexion in top shape

1. Cleansing is essential to thoroughly remove soil, makeup, pollution, excess oil and dead surface cells that can make skin look flaky or dull.
2. Toning is necessary to help stimulate skin and temporarily shrink pores for a finer-textured look.
3. Moisturizing is vital to help replenish the skin's moisture supply and create a barrier against the drying effects of the environment. It also provides a smooth cushion to help makeup slip on easily, stay fresher longer. It's an absolute must for all but the oiliest skins.

Handle skin gently
- When applying treatment creams and lotions, always glide fingers upward and outward. Never tug, stretch or press downward.

Be extravagant with moisturizers
- Eye and throat areas are almost always dry and very susceptible to early lining. These areas generate little natural oil. And the eye area is especially vulnerable because the skin here is so thin — 1/50 inch! Touch ever so gently.

Reevaluate your skin type
- Just because you had oily skin in your twenties doesn't mean you still have it in your thirties. As your skin type gradually becomes drier, your skin care regimen must include adding more moisture.

Be aware of seasonal changes
- Skin becomes oilier in summer, drier in winter. If necessary, adjust your regimen to care for skin's seasonal needs.

Win the battle of the blemish!
- Once or twice a week, use a cleanser with scrubbing grains. Alternate it with, or use it instead of, a facial mask.

A cleanser with grains goes deep, to help clear away excess oils and bacteria before they can cause blemishes. And the grains are mildly abrasive scrubbers that effectively help unclog pores and wash away blackheads.

Make the Most of Makeup

Make up in the right light
- Natural light brings out true color. So for daytime, always try to apply makeup in natural light, to achieve the most natural effect. Or, just check your finished makeup in natural light.

Blend, blend, blend
- When applying foundation, powder, blush and eye colors, blend, smooth, stroke and brush until all the hard edges disappear, until the beautiful result looks like you, only much, much better!

Play up your good points!
- Don't worry about your bad points! Just keep in mind the basic color principle of light and dark when making up eyes, cheeks and lips: Light, bright or shiny color makes an area seem to come forward. Dark or matte color makes it seem to recede.

Harmonize blush, lip and nail colors
- Make your eye, blush, lip and nail colors work together. Don't match them exactly . . . but do keep blush, lip and nail shades in the same color family. Select eye makeup colors to complement — because today's makeup look plays up your whole face, not just your eyes or lips!

Coordinate color to your wardrobe
- Makeup is a great fashion accessory! Collect eye, blush, lip and nail colors the way some people collect scarves. Because the right makeup colors are just as important to create a totally attractive look.

Your Makeup Essentials . . .

The secret of a flawless complexion
- A creamy concealer stick is the well kept secret of many a flawless-looking complexion! In mere seconds, it swivels up and strokes on to help banish dark under-eye circles. Choose the concealer shade closest to your own skin tone.
- To conceal dark under-eye circles draw two lines of concealer at the lower edge of the dark area: one from outer edge of eye to center, the other from inner edge of eye to center. Gently, fingertip blend up into the dark area. Don't try to lighten the area drastically; it looks natural to have a slight shadowing there.

- To conceal blemishes and flaws lightly dot on concealer; fingertip blend.
- Two light applications of concealer are better than one heavy application. Follow with foundation makeup and powder.

Foundation basics

- If you tend to be heavy-handed, apply liquid foundation makeup with a barely damp makeup sponge.
- Minimize lines on a mature skin by wearing a light-textured, dewy foundation and makeup.
- When you tan, switch to a sheer, darker-toned foundation makeup. Ease back into fall by blending both shades together in your palm before applying. That way you still have the right shade while your tan fades.

Powder perfectly

- For dry or maturing skins, apply face powder very lightly. If you're heavy-handed, you'll emphasize lines.
- For oily skins, face powder is a must to combat shine.
- For very deep skin tones, select face powder shade carefully. If a shade is too light, it can make skin look chalky or grayish.

Cheeky colors of blush

- Choose from earthy browns, romantic mauves, glowing burgundies, rosy-ripe pinks and vivid, clear reds. Experiment! A color you never thought of may give you an exciting new look, plus open up a whole new range of wardrobe possibilities. The key is coordinating blush color to clothing color.

- Naturally high-chiseled cheekbones take beautifully to brighter colors, too!
- You need more vibrant blush color when you wear black, or under artificial night lights.
- To intensify color, just add a little more blush. Build color gradually . . . it's easier to add than to take away.
- Use 2 products together to create your own special effects: Blush cheeks with soft, non-frosted color. Then stroke a little frost stick just over tops of cheekbones for a subtle, shimmery accent. Or . . . try powder over cream for a super-lasting blush.

Eyes are a most important asset!

- *Slightly* thinner brows make eyes look larger. No pencil-thin brows, please!
- Try two brow-coloring shades together for a naturally-blended look.
- When selecting your favorite eye shadow colors, keep in mind that light or frosted colors emphasize an area, while dark or matte colors minimize it.
- A smokey shadow shade blended all around eyes makes dark under-eye circles less noticeable.
- If you like a highlight shade, try beige or peach for a soft, naturally bright-eyed look.
- Deep, muted, earthy colors complement very deep skin tones. (Create evening drama with deep, but more vibrant, colors.)

Lashes . . . think lavish!

- For extra length, apply mascara to lash tip using only the tip of the brush.
- Curling lashes before applying mascara gives eyes a really wide-awake look! And if you wear glasses, it keeps your eyelashes from hitting the lenses. (Crimp the eyelash curler gently — too much pressure can break lashes.)
- For extra-thick lashes, dust with a little face powder between coats of mascara.
- Almost everyone's eyelashes wear basic black beautifully. But if you're really fair, you might prefer the softer look of brown for day. And save the drama of black for night.

For Luscious Lips . . .

- For more definition, outline lips with a *slightly* deeper lip color.
- Try a *tinted* gloss over lipstick or pencil to custom-blend your own extra-gleamy color.
- Brighter, shinier shades make lips look fuller while deeper, more muted shades make them look thinner.

Some Facts about Hairstyle . . .

Work with your hair, not against it.

- Choose styles that take advantage of your hair's natural tendencies — curly or straight. (Unless you've had your hair permed or straightened.)

The right cut is basic

- Blunt cuts add body and fullness (terrific for fine, straight hair). Layer cuts make the most of natural wave or curl.

Be realistic about style upkeep

- How well can you handle your hair? How much time are you willing to spend on styling?
- To help your hairstyle stay neatly in place all day (resist humidity, too) . . . lightly mist it with hair spray after styling.

Look in a full-length mirror

- Check the total proportion — how your hairstyle relates to your whole body.

Handcare

Keep your hands in lovely condition

- Push cuticles back with a towel when you dry your hands.
- A few times a week, apply cuticle conditioner and massage over base and sides of nails. (It won't affect your nail enamel.)
- Keep an emery board with you always, to smooth out chips and splits as soon as they occur.
- And help prevent breakage by using pads of fingers for buttons and zippers, knuckles on light switches and elevator buttons. Dial the telephone with a pencil, too.
- Moisturizing emollient creams or lotions help soften, smooth and soothe rough, dry skin. Use them daily, after washing your hands and at bedtime.

Lo-Cal Desserts

Peanut Butter Cookies

⅔ cup sifted flour
½ teaspoon baking soda
½ teaspoon baking powder
¼ teaspoon salt
6 tablespoons peanut butter
½ cup granulated sugar substitute concentrate
2 eggs

Preheat oven to 375°. Lightly grease cookie sheet. Sift together dry ingredients. Combine peanut butter and eggs. Add sugar concentrate substitute and mix well. Thoroughly mix in dry ingredients. Drop by teaspoonfuls onto cookie sheet. Flatten with tines of fork. Bake 10 to 12 minutes or until done. Makes 32 cookies. Each cookie is 26 calories.

Chocolate-Nut Brownies

1 square unsweetened chocolate
⅓ cup butter
2 tablespoons liquid sweetener or 48 tablets, crushed
2 teaspoons vanilla
2 eggs, beaten
1 cup sifted cake flour
½ teaspoon salt
½ teaspoon baking soda
¾ cup chopped walnuts

Melt the unsweetened chocolate and butter in a saucepan over low heat. Remove from heat. Add sweetener, vanilla, and the beaten eggs. Stir until well blended. Add sifted cake flour, salt, and baking soda. Mix until blended. Stir in the chopped walnuts. Pour into a greased 8-inch square pan. Level batter in pan. Bake in a slow 325° oven for 20 minutes. Cool. Cut into bars. Makes 32 brownies, 55 calories each.

Diet Dotted Cookies

¾ cup sugar
½ cup margarine
1 teaspoon coconut flavoring
3 tablespoons skim milk
1½ cups sifted flour
½ teaspoon baking powder
½ teaspoon salt
¾ cup coarsely chopped cranberries, drained
½ cup shredded coconut

Cream sugar, margarine and coconut flavoring until fluffy. Add milk, mixing well. Sift together flour, baking powder and salt. Add to sugar mixture. Fold berries into batter. Divide dough in half. Roll each half into a log about 1½ inches in diameter. Roll each log in shredded coconut. Wrap each log in waxed paper and chill 8 hours. Slice thin. Place on ungreased cookie sheet. Bake in a 375° oven 12 to 15 minutes. Makes 60 cookies. Each cookie is 39 calories.

Chocolate Creme Chiffon

¼ cup cocoa
1 tablespoon unflavored gelatin
1½ cups skim milk
3 egg yolks, slightly beaten
3 egg whites, beaten
¾ cup sugar substitute
⅛ teaspoon salt
1 teaspoon vanilla
¼ teaspoon cream of tartar

Combine cocoa and gelatin in the top of a double boiler. Gradually add skim milk, egg yolks, sugar substitute, and salt. Cook over boiling water, stirring constantly, until gelatin is dissolved and mixture is slightly thickened. Stir in vanilla. Chill until mixture thickens but does not set. Beat egg whites with cream of tartar until stiff but not dry. Fold in cocoa mixture thoroughly. Turn into 4-cup ring mold or individual molds. Chill until firm. Serves 8. Each serving is 77 calories.

Pumpkin Spice Torte

2½ cups sifted cake flour
3 teaspoons baking powder
2 teaspoons pumpkin pie spice
½ teaspoon cinnamon
½ teaspoon butter-flavored salt
6 egg yolks
⅔ cup diet margarine
1 cup canned pumpkin
¾ cup brown sugar, firmly packed
Sugar substitute to equal ⅔ cup sugar
6 egg whites
½ teaspoon cream of tartar

Sift together first 5 ingredients. Set aside. Combine yolks, diet margarine, pumpkin, brown sugar, and sugar substitute; beat until smooth. Gradually add dry mixture to pumpkin mixture, mixing well. Beat egg whites and cream of tartar until stiff. Gently fold pumpkin mixture into egg whites. Pour into a greased 10-inch non-stick tube pan. Bake in a 325° oven 60 minutes. Invert pan on rack to cool. Serves 16. Each serving contains 160 calories.

Cranberry Delight

    1 envelope unflavored gelatin
¼ cup cold water
    1 pint cranberry juice cocktail
    1 teaspoon liquid sweetener

Soften gelatin in cold water for 5 minutes. Heat cranberry cocktail thoroughly. Add gelatin and stir to dissolve. Add sweetener. Pour into 5 individual molds. Chill. Each serving contains 65 calories. Makes 6 servings.

Pecan Surprise Dessert

    3 egg whites
¼ cup nonfat dry milk
¼ cup ice water
¾ cup granulated sugar substitute
    1 teaspoon baking powder
½ teaspoon baking soda
    1 teaspoon vanilla
¾ cup finely chopped pecans
20 snack crackers, crumbled

Whip egg whites, dry milk and ice water until stiff peaks form. Add sugar substitute, baking powder, soda and vanilla. Fold in pecans and cracker crumbs. Spread in a lightly buttered 9-inch pie pan. Bake in a 350° oven 15 to 20 minutes. Serves 12 at 95 calories each serving.

Cherry Cobbler

    2 cups (1-pound can) water-packed cherries
      (drained, save juice)
    1 teaspoon cornstarch
½ teaspoon lemon juice
⅛ teaspoon almond flavoring
¼ teaspoon liquid sweetener
⅔ cup (about) cherry juice
½ cup sifted cake flour
¾ teaspoon baking powder
⅛ teaspoon salt
    1 tablespoon margarine or butter
    2 tablespoons blended egg
    2 tablespoons skim milk
½ teaspoon liquid sweetener

Place drained cherries in 8-inch pie pan or shallow cake pan. Combine juice drained from cherries, cornstarch, lemon juice, ¼ teaspoon sweetener, and almond flavoring in a saucepan. Heat until slightly thickened. Pour over cherries. Mix together dry ingredients. Cut in the shortening until mixture is almost granular. Add milk and ½ teaspoon sweetener to egg. Stir into dry ingredients. Drop onto cherries, making four biscuits. Bake at 425° about 25 to 30 minutes. Serve warm. Makes 4 servings. One serving is 155 calories.

Orange Sherbet

    1 14-ounce can evaporated milk, well chilled
    2 tablespoons liquid artificial sweetener
    1 6-ounce can unsweetened frozen orange juice
      concentrate, thawed

Beat evaporated milk, slightly. Gradually add sweetener and orange juice. Blend well. Freeze. One cup equals 140 calories. Yield: 3 pints.

Strawberry Pie

½ cup water
½ cup instant non-fat dry milk powder
    4 eggs
¼ teaspoon salt
½ cup sugar
¼ cup flour
    1 tablespoon lemon juice
    1 teaspoon vanilla
    1 1-pound container small curd cottage cheese
    1 quart whole strawberries
    1 9-inch graham cracker crust

Combine first 9 ingredients; blend until smooth. Pour into crust. Bake at 250° 60 minutes. Turn off heat and leave pie in oven 60 minutes. Remove and cool. Arrange berries on top and brush with Glaze. Each serving contains 177 calories. Serves 10.

Glaze

    1 tablespoon cornstarch
    1 cup water
      Liquid artificial sweetener
      Red food coloring

In a saucepan, combine cornstarch and water. Cook over low heat, stirring constantly, until thickened and clear. Add liquid sweetener to taste. Stir in a few drops red food coloring. Cool slightly.

Applesauce Cake

    2 cups raisins
    2 cups water
    1 cup unsweetened applesauce
    2 eggs
¾ cup vegetable oil
    2 tablespoons artificial sweetener
    2 cups flour
    1 teaspoon baking soda
1¼ teaspoons cinnamon
½ teaspoon nutmeg

Cook raisins in water until soft; drain. Add applesauce, eggs, oil and sweetener to raisins. Mix well. Add remaining ingredients. Mix well. Pour into a 9 x 13-inch glass pan greased with diet margarine. Bake in a 325° oven 45 minutes. 216 calories per serving. Serves 16.

Kids in the Kitchen

Children can be one of your most efficient time-savers in meal preparation. They will feel quite proud to say "I helped with dinner tonight!" Let them set the table or pick flowers for a pretty centerpiece. Kids can be quite creative in putting together salads if aided with the necessary chopping. Here are a few recipes complete with safety instructions that children can easily follow . . . and adults can enjoy!

Do's and Don'ts in the Kitchen

1 No bumped heads, please! Always close cabinet doors.

2 Sharp knives seen not felt. Always ask an adult to help you if you need to use a sharp knife.

3 Ouch! A burned finger! Remember to use hot pads.

4 Cutting boards are made for cutting — please don't use the counter or tabletop.

5 Use paper towels to wipe up any spill — so nobody slips and falls.

6 Keep your work space neat. You'll find it's easier to work when everything is in order.

7 Always remember to turn off the oven and burners when you are finished cooking.

8 Make sure that your hands are dry before using electrical appliances.

9 Before you start making any recipe, be sure to read it all the way through. Check to see that you have all the ingredients, the right size pots and pans, and then begin.

10 When you are finished cooking, be sure to clean up and put everything back in its place.

Never A Flop!

1 Measure ingredients properly and accurately using standard measuring cups and spoons.

2 Bake at the temperature specified in the recipe.

3 Use the size pan called for in the recipe.

4 Let ingredients sit at room temperature for a few minutes before using.

Caution!

1 Check with an adult before starting to cook. You must ask permission!

2 Make sure an adult is in the house while you are cooking.

3 Keep younger brothers and sisters away from your cooking area.

Funny Face Pancakes

You Will Need:

> griddle
> 2 medium mixing bowls
> liquid and dry
>   measuring cups
> measuring spoons
> pancake turner
> sifter
> rubber spatula
> wooden spoon
> small custard cup
> fork

Ingredients for Regular Pancakes:

> ¾ cup cornmeal
> 1¼ cups pancake mix
> 4 teaspoons sugar
> 1 egg
> 1¾ cups milk

Ingredients for Chocolate Pancakes:

> ¾ cup cornmeal
> 1¼ cups pancake mix
> 3 tablespoons cocoa
> ⅓ cup sugar
> 1 egg
> 1¾ cups milk

Before You Start:

Have adult show you how to use griddle. If electric, preheat griddle to 400°.

Steps to Follow for Regular Pancakes:

1. Measure cornmeal, pancake mix and sugar into sifter and sift into mixing bowl.
2. Beat egg slightly in custard cup.
3. Add egg and milk to dry ingredients and stir to combine.

Steps To Follow for Chocolate Pancakes:

1. Measure cornmeal, pancake mix, cocoa and sugar into sifter and sift into mixing bowl.
2. Beat egg slightly in custard cup.
3. Add egg and milk to dry ingredients and stir to combine.

To Make Funny Faces:

1. Drizzle some of the chocolate pancake batter from a teaspoon onto the hot griddle to form a face (two eyes and a smile, just as in the picture).
2. When bubbles form on the chocolate batter, pour ¼ cup of the regular batter over the face.
3. Turn the entire pancake over when the top of the pancake is covered with bubbles and the edges look dry.
4. Brown the other side, about 1 or 2 minutes.
5. Serve with butter and syrup. About 20 pancakes.

Mini Pizzas

You Will Need:

> cookie sheet
> measuring spoons
> pancake turner
> dinner knife
> can opener
> pot holders

Ingredients:

> 6 English muffins
> 1 10½-ounce can pizza sauce
> 1 3½-ounce package pepperoni
> 1 4-ounce can mushroom stems and pieces, drained
> 1 8-ounce package shredded pizza cheese

Before You Start:

Preheat oven to 400°.

Steps To Follow:

1. Split muffins in half.

2. Lay muffin halves cut side up on a cookie sheet.
3. Spread about 1 tablespoon pizza sauce on each half.
4. Top with pepperoni slices and mushrooms.
5. Sprinkle cheese on top.
6. Place in preheated 400° oven.
7. Remove with pancake turner and serve immediately. 12 mini pizzas.

Frankfurter Casserole

You Will Need:

2-quart casserole
pot holders
rubber spatula
measuring spoons
small frying pan
tongs
paper toweling
cutting board
knife
can opener

Ingredients:

4 slices bacon
1 10¾-ounce can condensed cream of mushroom soup
1 tablespoon instant minced onion
½ teaspoon salt
1 8-ounce can peas, drained
1 16-ounce can whole kernel corn, drained
1 15-ounce can sliced potatoes, drained
6 frankfurters, sliced crosswise

Before You Start:

Preheat oven to 350°. Have adult help you slice frankfurters into coins and slice bacon into ½-inch pieces.

Steps To Follow:

1. Place bacon pieces in small frying pan.
2. Fry over medium heat until crisp.
3. Remove bacon and place on paper toweling to drain. Set aside.
4. Place soup, onion, and salt in 2-quart casserole.
5. Stir in peas, corn, potatoes and sliced frankfurters.
6. Sprinkle bacon over the top.
7. Place in preheated 350° oven and set timer for 45 minutes. 6 servings.

Ice Cream Cart

You Will Need:

knife
cutting board

Ingredients:

1 pint brick ice cream
8 animal cookies
16 gingersnaps or vanilla wafers

Before You Start:

Place 4 small plates in the refrigerator to chill. Have adult help you cut ice cream into 4 equal slices.

Steps To Follow:

1. Place each ice cream slice on a chilled plate.
2. Stand 2 animal cookies up in front of each ice cream slice.
3. Make "wheels" along both sides of ice cream slices with the cookies.
4. Serve right away or freeze until ready to serve. 4 Ice Cream Carts.

Funny Face Pancakes, p. 77. Mini Pizzas, p. 77
Frankfurter Casserole. Ice Cream Cart

Kids in the Kitchen 79

Index